Heroes, Scoundrels and Angels

Heroes, Scoundrels and Angels

Fairview Cemetery of Gainesville, Texas

Ron Melugin

The History Press

Published by The History Press
Charleston, SC 29403
www.historypress.net

Back cover: Funeral scene courtesy of George J. Carroll & Son Funeral Home.
Unless otherwise noted, all images are by the author.

First published 2010

Manufactured in the United States

ISBN 978.1.60949.033.1

Library of Congress Cataloging-in-Publication Data
Melugin, Ron.
Heroes, scoundrels, and angels : Fairview Cemetery of Gainesville, Texas / Ron Melugin.
p. cm.
Includes bibliographical references and index.
ISBN 978-1-60949-033-1
1. Fairview Cemetery (Gainesville, Tex.) 2. Gainesville (Tex.)--Biography. 3. Sepulchral monuments--Texas--Gainesville. 4. Inscriptions--Texas--Gainesville. 5. Gainesville (Tex.)--Genealogy. 6. Registers of births, etc.--Texas--Gainesville. I. Title.
F394.G15M34 2010
363.7'509764533--dc22
2010030110

This labor of love is dedicated to my loving wife, Claudia.

"The past is not dead. It is not even past."
—William Faulkner

The author with grandson Sean Melugin preparing for the 150th anniversary of Fairview.

Contents

Division 4: Oldest Part of the Cemetery

Division 5

Division 6

Division 7: East of 6 and 6A

Division 18: People of Color

Division 18A

Division 19

Preface

There are over forty Fairview cemeteries in the United States. Fairview Cemetery in Gainesville, Texas, is unique, as all others are, if for no other reason than that its "residents" are unique. This cemetery is a gold mine of local history, serving the living as well as the dead.

Tombstones serve as bookmarks to people's lives. You can take the death date from a tombstone and use that as a reference for looking up obituaries, death records and probate records. Those "bookmarks" may be simple; they may be ornate. They may be accurate; they may be inaccurate. Tombstone artisans may not have good information and may not be good spellers.

Cemetery records are also a good starting point, provided they exist and are accessible. Unmarked graves are obviously harder to research.

I have selected almost two hundred "residents" of Fairview out of approximately eighteen thousand of the deceased to highlight their stories. I picked persons who had either historical significance; unique, interesting life experiences; unusual causes of death; or unusual grave markers or epitaphs that the Fairview visitor may enjoy. The ones who have more lengthy narratives were ones I researched for Official Texas Historical Marker subjects; these are marked with the designation "THM."

My selection has been biased, affected by gaps in the microfilm record of the *Gainesville Hesperian* and the *Gainesville Register*. My research has been happenstance. The reader may know someone who you think should have been included. If so, that is your opportunity to do some writing.

I am indebted to the following people, without whose help this book would have been impossible: the Cross Timbers Genealogical Society, which published an inventory of graves in Fairview Cemetery in 1985; the staff of Fairview Cemetery and sextons, the late John Smallwood, Craig Evins and Dusty Luton; Cooke County Library librarians and staffs of the late Ann Woods and Jennifer Johnson-Spence; North Central Texas College (NCTC) former director of library services, Patsy Wilson, and current director, Dianne Roether, and their staffs, including Sharon Simmons, Cecilia Hoenig, Sharon Kirkpatrick and Shedrick Pittman-Hassett, who helped or patiently listened to my stories; and my wife, Claudia, who is a frequent, temporary "cemetery widow." Susie McDonald helped me with some local history research. Joe Carroll of the George Carroll & Son family told me some of his cemetery "secrets" shortly before his death in 1995, and Buddy Sisson has helped me with funeral records. Dan Flint Jr. is also an excellent source of funeral lore. I am also thankful for the congenial staffs of Cooke County District Court Clerk Pat Payne and of Cooke County Clerk Rebecca Lawson.

Others who have helped me with my research include Randel Beaver, Tom Carson, Jim O'Bryant, the late Marjorie Powell and Gene Shasteen. I am indebted to my North Central Texas College colleagues and friends, Dr. Ron Bost and Sara Flusche, who helped me with my map graphics. I would be remiss in not mentioning my other friends and colleagues who also patiently listened to my stories: Jack Cable, Jim Crump, Dan Doss, Cliff Downey, Eddie Hadlock, Pat Ledbetter, Lynn Peters, Ann Norcross and Crystal Wright.

Ona B. Reed, former chair of the Cooke County Historical Commission, has always been an inspiration to me on my various historical projects. Gerron Hite, recently retired from the Texas Historical Commission Historic Cemeteries Program, taught me the proper way to clean a tombstone. This book would never have happened if the late Joe Stout, longtime Gainesville Junior High history teacher and adjunct history instructor for NCTC, had not infected me with an appreciation of cemeteries as a classroom. My commissioning editor at The History Press, Becky LeJeune, has been gracious and prompt in dealing with any of my publishing hurdles.

Division 1

Killed Over a Twenty-five-Cent Debt

John Grimes (buried on December 24, 1889), a local gunsmith, was accidentally killed in a fight over a dispute involving a difference of opinion on whether a customer of his, A.H. Jones, owed him twenty-five cents on a gun repair.

The fatal fight occurred about ten o'clock in the evening at the saloon of Waterman and Friedenheit on Commerce Street. Grimes was drinking beer at the bar when A.H. Jones, owner of a furniture store on North Dixon, came up to the bar to order a drink. Grimes remarked that he owed him twenty-five cents for a gun repair. Jones claimed he had paid the bill in full. Grimes hit Jones in the face, knocking him down. Jones got up, and the two went at it. In the melee, Jones tripped Grimes, and Grimes fell backward, hitting the back of his head on the edge of a whisky barrel lying nearby.

Grimes's neck was broken near the base of his skull. Death was instantaneous. When Jones was informed of that fact, "he broke down and wept like a child. He ordered the bartender to bath [sic] Grimes' breast with whisky and place mustard plasters over the vital parts, which was readily done, but to no avail." A reporter of the *Daily Hesperian* who was an eyewitness wrote the newspaper account. (MAP: JG)

Three Burials from One Household in Three Days

This account is based on a story told by an anonymous friend of **Sophia A. (Ringold) Stone** (November 2, 1826—January 10, 1892) in the *National Christian Advocate* and reprinted in the *Hesperian*. **Dr. J.B. Stone** (1822–January 11, 1892) and his wife, Sophia, and brother **D. Webb Stone** (1834–January 9, 1892) lived together at Sivells Bend.

On April 28, 1845, Dr. Stone of Henry County, Virginia, and Sophia Ringold, a native of Batesville, Arkansas, were united in marriage. They moved to Sivells Bend in 1859.

On January 9, 1892, Webb Stone died at their Sivells Bend home. Mrs. Stone died early the next day of *la grippe*. Webb's and Sophia Stone's caskets lay side by side for the funeral service at the Methodist Episcopal Church, South in Gainesville. Dr. Stone and one son were too ill to attend the services.

After the funeral, the children of Sophia and Dr. Stone rushed to his bedside at Sivells Bend. One of those children, according to another *Hesperian* article, was Mrs. Conson, who "had made a lonely journey from the far off Pacific coast," and the "strain upon heart and nerve called forth the sympathy of every one who knew her."

The children found Dr. Stone in his bed praying to quickly follow his wife and brother to heaven. His prayer was answered early the next morning when "he joined his wife and brother on the other side of death's dark river." (MAP: ST)

Noted Ornithologist and Naturalist

G.H. (George Henry) Ragsdale (April 1, 1846–March 25, 1895), a man of little formal education, became a well-respected source of information on geology, birds and natural history. Ragsdale was born in Knox County, Tennessee, and according to Stanley D. Castro in his entry on Ragsdale in *The Handbook of Texas Online*, his formal schooling probably ended with the Civil War.

He is buried with two wives. **Elizabeth Letitia Owens** (March 9, 1847–July 11, 1881) from Knoxville, Tennessee, died from complications during childbirth. Ragsdale married **Kitty Brewster Reinhardt** (1859–February

1941) in 1883. He had two sons from his first marriage and four children from his second marriage. Vic Reinhardt, Kitty's brother, a Terrell journalist for the temperance movement, inspired Ragsdale to submit articles for that cause to his publication, *Temperance Vedette.*

Ragsdale came to Cooke County in 1867, where he took up farming southeast of Gainesville. In the 1870s, he was county surveyor, and that job gave him the opportunity for astute observation of the outdoors. He became a serious collector of birds and their eggs, wrote regular commentaries in the *Gainesville Hesperian*, corresponded with the Smithsonian Institution and was cited in numerous scholarly works. He acquired a collection of six hundred eggs and was a prodigious taxidermist of birds. He supplemented his income as a farmer by taxidermy and selling specimens he had collected, according to Castro.

Here is a sample of the kind of inquiries Ragsdale submitted to the local paper: "Will you please say to my gunning friends that the white-fronted goose and the black mallard appear to be rare in Cooke County, and if they get either of these birds to please report same to G.H. Ragsdale."

In June 1893, he reported in the *Hesperian* that Robert T. Hill (whom he had assisted in his study) had recently printed a thirty-page pamphlet on the fossils of the Upper Cross Timbers or Trinity Division of the Lower Crustaceons of Texas. Hill had named a fossil oyster found in the Glen Rose area *ostrea franklini ragsdalei* in his honor. Castro also alludes to John Allen Singley's *Natural History of Texas* (1893), whose section on mollusks included numerous specimens provided by Ragsdale. Again, Ragsdale was honored with a snail specimen named for him, *Rabdotus dealbatus ragsdalei*, from the St. Jo area. (MAP: GR)

A Flour Mill and a Church

James O.A. Whaley (1845–August 1909), a native of Tennessee and Confederate army veteran, settled in the Fish Creek area in northwest Cooke County in 1866. After three years of skirmishing with Indians, he bought **John E. Wheeler's** (Division 2) mill on the east side of Gainesville. According to the *Handbook of Texas Online*, flour milling was the biggest industry in Texas prior to the Civil War. From 1882 until 1896, Whaley operated a steam-powered mill on Lindsay Street until an explosion ended that facility. His next mill operation was a mammoth one that stands vacant today adjacent to the Santa Fe Railroad tracks on Denison Street. In 1948, the Whaley Mill and Elevator Company was purchased by Fort Worth multimillionaire and art collector Kay Kimball. It came under the operation of Fant Milling Company of Sherman, whose product name was Gladiola Flour.

Whaley's father, **John Whaley** (1800–1867), a Methodist minister, and his mother, **Mary "Polly" Airheart Whaley** (1803–1880), had thirteen children. James, active in the Methodist Church all his life, became the namesake for Whaley United Methodist Church, which was renamed and relocated on the northwest corner of California and Grand in 1915 after the Broadway Street Methodist Church burned to the ground. That church was preceded by a mission church dating back to 1887. Whaley Church was forced to rebuild and relocate to 701 Rosedale in Gainesville due to safety issues with its dome at its previous location in 1979.

The Whaley family burial plot also includes J.O.A.'s wife, **Mary I. Whaley** (1845–April 1926), and two babies. (MAP: WH)

Holland's Magazine Columnist

Ellie V. (Mrs. John) Turner (1862–November 5, 1939) died after a brief illness in her home in Dallas. She had lived in Dallas for over forty years. Ellie had a regular children's column under the name of "Aunt Wilmena" in *Holland's Magazine* for a number of years. M.W. Holland, publisher of the magazine, was one of her pallbearers.

In the current issue of *Holland's* at the time of her death, she had a page devoted to the Gainesville Community Circus and invited young readers to participate in an essay contest on the subject of the circus. *Holland's Magazine* was published under this name from 1905 until 1952 by the Texas Farm and Ranch Publishing Company of Dallas. (MAP: ET)

Division 2

Infant of County Official, Turned Train Robber

An infant of E.F. Bunch lies in Division 2 in an unmarked grave. According to the cemetery records, the infant was buried on March 4, 1879. That burial occurred at the time Bunch was Cooke County clerk.

The story of E.F. Bunch is both puzzling and fascinating. He was born in Noxubee County, Mississippi, in 1843. His occupations were varied. He was a schoolteacher for a time in Amite, Louisiana. One of his students there, J. Leon Pounds, who had relatives in Gainesville, later became an accomplice of "Captain Bunch" in some stagecoach and train robberies. Bunch came to Gainesville prior to 1876. In 1876 and in subsequent elections of 1878 and 1880, he was elected and reelected county clerk.

According to one newspaper account, he left Gainesville around 1886 after being indicted for forgery. Around July 1888, Bunch returned to Gainesville and arranged a personal meeting with W.W. Howeth. Bunch admitted to passing three forged checks on Howeth's account for $400 each and promised to repay him. But that didn't happen.

Bunch was also suspected of being the "lone highwayman" who robbed the stagecoach between San Angelo and Ballinger on several occasions in 1888, although his former student was the stage-driver and "inside man" in those robberies.

According to the *New Orleans Times-Democrat*, as repeated in the *Gainesville Hesperian*, on November 3, 1888, Bunch (alias "J.H. Gerald or Girard") robbed the express car of the Northeastern Railroad between Derby and Lacey, Louisiana, of approximately $30,000. Bunch carried two revolvers and was bold and efficient. This was not his first train robbery because there was already a $1,000 reward posted for Bunch, described as six feet, three inches tall, slightly stoop-shouldered and weighing 195 pounds.

Bunch eluded capture, but his two accomplices, J. Leon Pounds and a female friend who used the alias Mrs. Cora Ellis, were captured shortly after the robbery. The female accomplice had $1,200 sewed into her clothing and was carrying two revolvers and dynamite cartridges.

Although Bunch had been a married man with children while in Gainesville, according to *Pictorial History of the Wild West*, Bunch was quite a ladies' man and circulated well in Dallas social circles. His last love—and it is unclear whether this was "Mrs. Ellis" or someone else—was the daughter of a former governor of Texas.

In 1889, Bunch put together a gang of desperadoes and headed for Mississippi. A posse led by Pinkerton detective Charles O. Summers and another detective for the Southern Express located Bunch and a couple of his men on an island deep in a swamp in Jefferson County, Mississippi. Summers shot and killed Bunch while trying to escape after two of his companions in crime had been fatally shot. (MAP: IB)

WHEELER CREEK NAMED FOR THIS PIONEER

John E. Wheeler (October 28, 1801–December 13, 1880), Methodist minister and farmer, came to Gainesville in 1857. He was born in Campbell City, Tennessee. According to A. Morton Smith, he built the first two-story building in the county and constructed a mule-powered flour mill on the creek east of Gainesville that would eventually bear his name. **James O.A. Whaley** (Division 1) later bought Wheeler's mill. Wheeler bought the 300 block of South Commerce and moved to town when his sons joined the Confederacy. (MAP: JW)

Parents of Pioneer Surgeon

Rufus Franklin Scott (June 3, 1828–December 31, 1905) and **Martha Helen Moran Scott** (December 25, 1833–February 28, 1901) were the parents of Arthur Carroll Scott (1865–1940), a pioneer in cancer surgery and founder of Scott and White Memorial Hospital in Temple. After attending rural schools in Cooke County, Scott started studying under **Dr. A.H. Conson** (Division 15) at the age of seventeen. From 1882 until 1886, he studied at Bellevue Medical College in New York, where he received his MD degree.

He returned to practice medicine in Gainesville in 1888 until his promotion as chief surgeon for the Santa Fe Railroad required him to relocate in Temple at the Santa Fe Hospital. In 1894, he hired Dr. Raleigh White as a surgeon, and they established a hospital and nursing school that became Scott and White Memorial Hospital in 1922.

Dr. Scott's primary contributions to the field of medicine were in the field of cancer diagnosis and surgery. One of his innovations was the use of the hot cautery knife in cancer surgery. He was known nationally and internationally for his medical advances. According to Paxton Howard in the *Handbook of Texas Online*, the primary source for this entry, "Scott and White Hospital [also] pioneered concepts…in industrial medicine, multispecialty group practice, prepaid health insurance, and postgraduate medical education." (MAP: SC)

Rufus Scott also has an interesting connection to **Bob Scott** in Division 18.

This Marker Speaks for Itself

This inscription is on a tablet marker that is lying on the ground, and it features two clasped hands at the top: **MARY A.** Wife of **N.A. STROUBE**. Born February 28, 1860; Died August 22, 1884. (MAP: MS)

But those lips that echoed the sound of mine
Are as cold as that lonely river,
And that eye that beautiful spirits shrine
Has shrouded its fires forever.

Appointed Special Surveyor by President John Quincy Adams

Colonel James W. Drake (November 21, 1803–October 3, 1888), according to the *Gainesville Hesperian*, Colonel Drake spent the last ten years of his life moving back and forth between Texas and Mississippi among his children, grandchildren and great-grandchildren.

Drake was born in Nash County, North Carolina, in 1803. He was appointed a special surveyor by President John Quincy Adams to survey a piece of land that was a gift to Marquis de Lafayette, American Revolutionary hero. Lafayette was in the United States for fourteen months, at the end of President Monroe's term and the beginning of John Quincy Adams's presidency.

Drake was an "extensive letter writer." Among those with whom he corresponded was Lyman Draper (1815–1891), a well-known archivist and historian of the Trans-Allegheny West who contributed greatly to the University of Wisconsin historical collection, and former Confederate general and longtime leader of Freemasonry in the South, Albert Pike. At the time of Drake's death, he had been a Mason for sixty-two years and was the oldest Mason in the Gainesville lodge. (MAP: JD)

Knights of Pythias

Andrew A. Carrington (June 19, 1871–June 22, 1893), grandson-in-law of **Colonel Drake**, was born in Hardeman County, Tennessee. He was a railroad conductor and died of meningitis. He was a member of the Knights of Pythias. Many prominent Gainesvilleites were members of this fraternal organization. In January 1888, N.C. Snider placed this notice in the *Gainesville Hesperian*: "Will the person who borrowed his Knights of Pythias sword and belt last summer to use on parade, please return same?" In 1928, the old Gainesville Opera House was converted to the Pythian Castle Hall on the northwest corner of Rusk and Main. Carrington's columnar grave marker features the Knights of Pythias emblem with the helmeted head of a knight and a skull and crossbones. The skull and crossbones have not always had an exclusive pirate's image. The "F," "C" and "B" on the monument stand for "friendship," "charity" and "benevolence."

The skull and crossbones are part of the Knights of Pythias symbol on the grave marker of Andrew Carrington. The Knights of Pythias was a fraternal organization endorsed by President Abraham Lincoln.

The Knights of Pythias was founded by Justus H. Rathbone on February 19, 1864, in Washington, D.C. President Lincoln promoted this organization as a way of helping reunite the North and the South after the Civil War. The Knights of Pythias is based on a Greek story about a friend who volunteered to take his friend's place in being executed because he didn't want his married friend's wife to become a widow. Marker inscription:

Let us pledge unto each other
Charity, Truth and Love
And we ne'er shall lack a brother
And at last shall meet above.
(MAP: AC)

Fratricide on the Courthouse Square

Homer Gibson (d. October 14, 1918), an eighteen-year-old boy, was shot to death by his forty-year-old brother, C.B. "Brad" Gibson, on the courthouse square. Homer was walking west on Main Street. Homer, a member of the local cavalry troop, had just come from the cavalry armory on the south side of the square, accompanied by his friend, Jess Griffith. Brad Gibson emerged from the Gibson undertaking parlor and shot his younger brother in the back with number 8 shot from a double-barreled shotgun from a distance of approximately twenty-five feet. He shot a second time, missing him. He was in the act of reloading when his brother ran a short distance west on Main Street and fell. When it was determined that Homer was mortally wounded, he was carried unconscious into Gibson's undertaking establishment, where he died a few minutes later.

Brad Gibson immediately surrendered to Will Ross and Henry Frasher. The shooting was apparently premeditated. Brad had rented the shotgun from H.F. Smith minutes before the shooting. Observers say there was a long-standing family feud. Several days before the shooting, another Gibson brother beat up Brad, while Homer kept a crowd from intervening. A jury in district court found Brad "not guilty" on grounds that his brother had previously threatened him and participated in assaulting him. (MAP: HG)

Division 3

Morris Family: Unique Grave Marker

As you turn into the main gate of Fairview, on the near right close to the front fence is a picturesque grave marker that depicts two children inside a shell. This marks the grave of the **Edwin T. Morris** (1840–March 11, 1910) family, also including his wife, **Martha E. Davenport Morris** (1847–March 8, 1910), and children, **Ira** (d. July 29, 1877; age one year, two months, eighteen days days) and **Mary** (d. October 30, 1883; age nine years, two months, nine days). The Morrises lived at Horseshoe Bend on Red River.

Edwin had been a captain in the Confederacy, and he was elected to one term as sheriff of Cooke County in 1874. He was also a stockholder in Red River Cattle Company. Notice that he and his wife died three days apart. They died of erysipelas, also called "St. Anthony's Fire." This was a streptococcal infection that first affected the skin and then the lymphatic system, the joints and the valves of the heart. (MAP: MO)

Moved to Cooke County to Escape Indians

Rachel Gibbs Allbright Freeman Gilbert (1827–December 23, 1894) was the second wife and widow of prominent North Texas pioneer Mabel Gilbert, who is included in the *Handbook of Texas Online*. Rachel, a twenty-

In Division 3, this little angel marks the grave of Lady Edith Rumrill, who did not quite reach her third birthday in 1883.

eight-year-old widow with one child, married Gilbert—who was thirty-one years her senior—in Grayson County on December 18, 1855. Her husband, who in his earlier years had been a Mississippi River steamboat captain, brought eleven children to this marriage. Prior to his marriage to Rachel, his pioneering spirit had led him all over North Texas to Fannin County, Tarrant County, Dallas County to John Neely Bryan's settlement and Grayson County. After his marriage to Rachel, they moved to what would become Wichita County. There, Rachel gave birth to the first Anglo baby born in Wichita County.

They later retreated to Montague County to escape Indian threats and moved back to Wichita County in 1867, where they farmed in an area that would become part of the Burkburnett oilfield. When Mabel died of pneumonia in early 1870, Rachel moved her family to a farm south of

These two children enclosed by a shell represent the eternal innocence of Sheriff Ed Morris's children of the late nineteenth century.

Gainesville. Her fear of Indians prompted this move. A short time later, she gave birth to Mabel's twenty-first child, a girl named Mabel.

In her later years, Rachel Gilbert was known as "Grandma Gilbert." (MAP: RG)

Division 4

Oldest Part of the Cemetery

A Cemetery Tour Should Start Here: The Howeth Family

The first graves in Fairview Cemetery are those of **Thomas B. Howeth**, eleven years old, and his sister, **Louisa M. Howeth**, nine years old, children of **William H. Howeth** (1818–1891) and **Hariette Bell Howeth** (1825–1908). The Howeths were among the first settlers in Cooke County, and the Howeth children were killed when a tornado struck the family cabin six miles west of Gainesville on May 28, 1854. Louisa's body was carried four miles by the tornado. The tornado also killed Andy Howeth and his two children in the same cabin. Thomas and Louisa are buried in a false crypt (bodies are below ground), which has a newer gray slab top that evidently replaced one that broke.

William H. Howeth, Tennessee native and owner of three slaves, was a member of Gainesville's "Great Hanging" jury in October 1862, which resulted in the deaths of forty-two people who were presumed to be members of a "Peace Party" that was perceived to threaten local authorities.

This cemetery originated as the Howeth family cemetery, and it was east of the city limits of Gainesville. William H. gave the original ten-acre cemetery to Cooke County "as a Christian duty and matter of public charity" on March 24, 1868. Two days after its tenth anniversary as a county cemetery, the Cooke County Commissioners Court turned the cemetery over to the City of Gainesville. It has remained city property since March 26, 1878.

Cara Melugin, granddaughter of the author, is singing "Down to the River to Pray" at the Howeth children's grave at the 150th anniversary of Fairview Cemetery.

William H. was a charter member of the first Masonic lodge, Lodge #210 of the Ancient Free and Accepted Masons (AF&AM), chartered in 1858. He also created the Howeth Title and Abstract Company in 1869, and this company continued under his son, **W.W. Howeth** (1847–1913). The abstract company remained in the Howeth family for over one hundred years. After the city acquired this cemetery, W.W. was paid twenty-five dollars to make a plat of the cemetery.

Harvey Howeth (October 1, 1821–September 26, 1898), according to Richard B. McCaslin's *Tainted Breeze: The Great Hanging at Gainesville, Texas, 1862*, was a member of the local militia who shot and killed Dr. James T. Foster, a condemned man, when he tried to escape the hangman's noose during the "Great Hanging" of 1862. Harvey's wife, **Susan A. Howeth** (June 11, 1829–May 12, 1913), received a pension after her husband's death due to his service in the Mexican War. (MAP: HO)

William Howeth, "out of Christian duty," gave his family cemetery to Cooke County, which in turn gave it to the City of Gainesville in 1878 in the form of a 999-year lease. *Courtesy of Morton Museum of Cooke County.*

Fought in the Battle of San Jacinto

It was by a historical accident that I determined that **Preston Conlee** (d. March 14, 1873) is buried in Fairview. His grave is one of numerous graves missing from Fairview records. Conlee's resting place is mentioned in *Those Buried Texans*, in the Cooke County Library. To prove that he is here, I found paperwork of his descendants at the Barker History Center at the University of Texas. His descendants had applied for membership in the Descendants of San Jacinto. I talked to one of his descendants, a resident of Oklahoma, on the phone. She said Preston Conlee had a wooden grave marker that was burned in a grass fire some years ago. There is one wooden grave marker that remains in Fairview, and it is near the Howeth family plot. I like to think of it as representing Preston Conlee, although we don't actually know whose grave it marks. Conlee's actual grave site is unknown.

Conlee entered the military service of Texas about September 1, 1835. According to land records, he possessed one-third of a league of land in Bastrop County. Conlee served as a private in Jesse Billingsley's company of the "Mina Volunteers" from the Bastrop area. This group became Company C of the First Regimental Infantry under Colonel Edward Burleson at the Battle of San Jacinto.

On February 2, 1839, he was appointed to a committee by the Bastrop city council to solicit land donations to help Bastrop lure the capital of the Republic of Texas to that location. Bastrop lost the competition to Waterloo, forty miles north. Conlee was sheriff of Bastrop County for approximately ten years, from 1839 to 1848 and from 1856 to 1858. In his later years, due to his declining health, he and his wife, **Martha E. Conlee** (buried Nov. 20, 1924) (Division 19), moved to Gainesville to be near their daughter, **Sue McKemie** (Division 19). (MAP: PC)

His Death Added to the Tension That Preceded the "Great Hanging"

James W. McCall (May 4, 1839–January 11, 1862) was owner of McCall's Saloon in Gainesville. McCall taunted a father and son in his saloon who had come to join the local militia and were brandishing new pocket knives, which they said they could use to kill Yankees, according to historian Richard McCaslin in *Tainted Breeze*. McCall made fun of their boast, and the father and son retaliated by fatally stabbing him. Friends of McCall didn't waste time in taking the two out of jail and promptly hanged them in front of McCall's Saloon.

James McCall has an interesting tombstone considering that he was a saloon owner. It is a round-topped tablet, broken and lying on the ground. It features a lamb lying under a weeping willow tree. The lamb is a common symbol for innocence that is usually featured on the tombstone of a child. His grave is a short distance east of the Howeth family plot. (MAP: JM)

He Deserves Better than This

William Thomas Green Weaver (commonly called **W.T.G. Weaver**) was born in Carolton, Illinois, on April 25, 1832. He died of an apparent heart attack while walking on the Cooke County courthouse square on October 18, 1876. Weaver was one of Cooke County's most talented and fascinating nineteenth-century leaders whose influence went well beyond Cooke County. "He deserves better than this" refers to the broken tombstone lying on his grave, although he is properly recognized with an Official Texas Historical Marker on Weaver Street in front of Gainesville Civic Center.

Weaver's formal education was sporadic. He taught school for a while in Hopkins County and later in Rockwall. He also worked as a land office clerk in Alton, the original county seat of Denton County. He was a self-taught lawyer who was admitted to the bar in 1856 in McKinney. He migrated to Gainesville in 1857 and became a law partner of G.A. Evarts. In 1860, he was elected district attorney for the Twentieth Judicial District, which covered an eleven-county area.

Although he opposed secession, he resigned as district attorney in 1862 and became a private in the Confederate army under **Captain F.M. Dougherty**. A little more than two years later, Weaver was promoted to captain. For a while, he was a prisoner of war after the Battle of Pleasant Hill in Louisiana. He was released on a prisoner exchange and took over what was left of his company to fight again at the Battle of Jenkins Ferry in Arkansas. During the Civil War, Weaver wrote numerous sketches and poems under the title *Stray Leaves from a Soldier's Journal*. They were published in various newspapers in Texas, Louisiana and Mississippi.

After the war, Governor James Throckmorton—Throckmorton Street in Gainesville is probably named for him—appointed W.T.G. Weaver judge for the Twentieth Judicial District. He didn't stay judge for very long, because General Phil Sheridan removed Governor Throckmorton and many of his state district judges for being "impediments to reconstruction."

Weaver married **Nancy Wilkin Fletcher** (October 11, 1846–August 31, 1933) at his mother and father-in law's Fletcher Hotel, the first hotel in Gainesville. Weaver was an alcoholic, however, which led to a subsequent separation from his wife. One of their two sons, Claude, followed his father's footsteps as an attorney and eventually a United States representative-at-large for Oklahoma from 1913 to 1915. Claude Weaver, in his *Memoirs*, declared that his mother always loved his father although she couldn't live with him.

W.T.G. Weaver's travels throughout north central Texas as a practicing attorney contributed to his election as a delegate to the Texas Constitutional Convention of 1875, which produced our current state constitution. One of the goals of that convention was to reduce extravagant spending, which was a hallmark of state government during Reconstruction. Weaver and a majority of the delegates favored the elimination of the Bureau of Immigration, which had paid immigrants to come to Texas. Weaver declared he was not opposed to immigration to Texas but thought it was ridiculous for the state to advertise itself. His response was that everybody in the civilized world knew about Texas and that it was unnecessary to advertise at state expense.

Weaver was part of a small vocal minority at that convention who favored giving women the vote. He argued that Eve represented the mother, wife, sister and daughter who "has the first care of our lives, is our nurse in childhood, our mentor in youth, our companion, helper and consoler in manhood, our comforting, ministering and sustaining angel in death" and was "morally and mentally man's equal," and women should have "the same rights at the ballot-box man has."

One of the persons Weaver favorably impressed at the 1875 Constitutional Convention was young Temple Houston, son of Sam Houston. Temple served as a page at that convention. Later, as an up-and-coming attorney, he gave a glowing eulogy in honor of the deceased Weaver from the steps of the Cooke County Courthouse.

In 1876, in the year of his death, Weaver managed to publish much of the poetry he had written in his lifetime in a two-hundred-page volume entitled *Hours of Amusement.* Some of his writings were later included in Davis Foute Eagleton's *Writers and Writings of Texas*, published in 1913.

This narrative was written earlier to justify an Official Texas Historical Marker for W.T.G. Weaver.

Here is an excerpt from a humorous poem condemning female snuff dippers, from *Hours of Amusement*:

To the Fair Dippers
(Inscribed to the Anti-Tobacco Association)

Oh, can a fair girl of the South—
Like a rose that's just out of the bud,
Roll that snuff-colored mop in her mouth
Like a young heifer chewing her cud!

Oh, charming young damsels, refrain
From that vile, detestable stuff!
Never poison your dear lips again
With old cigars ground into snuff.

(MAP: WW)

Casualty of the Civil War

Sergeant W.H.H. Addington (October 17, 1840–January 3, 1862) is the only known casualty of the Civil War buried in Fairview. His tablet marker contains the following inscription:

This tablet marker is at the grave of Confederate Sergeant W.H.H. Addington, the only actual casualty of the Civil War in this cemetery. He was mortally wounded near Fort Gibson, Indian Territory.

> *born in Gilmer County, Georgia. He was wounded at the Battle of Oastanalla, Indian Territory on Dec. 26th 1861. Died at Fort Gibson 3 Jan. 1862. Interned* [sic] *at this place 4 Feb. 1862. Tell Mother I died for her and will meet her in Heaven.*

This battle is also known as "Chustenahlah" or "Patriot Hills." This battle involved a 1,400-man Confederate force of Texas and Arkansas cavalry under Colonel James McIntosh versus a Union Creek force led by Creek Chief Apothleyohola, aided by Seminoles, African Americans and Cherokee deserters from Colonel John Drew's First Cherokees Mounted Rifles. The battle occurred between the Verdigris and Arkansas Rivers in northeastern Indian Territory (Oklahoma). Apothleyohola, after receiving approximately 250 casualties compared to 3 Confederate casualties, retreated to Kansas. (MAP: WA)

Prominent Cattleman

Zach T. Addington (October 22, 1847–October 4, 1922) was a prominent rancher who ranched in the Comanche part of Indian Territory. Gainesville College, a coeducational college (not the later one of similar name), opened in his former home in the 1000 block of South Denton Street. In 1895, Paul Gallia bought the house, had it razed and materials from it became part of a new opera house at Rusk and Main, according to A. Morton Smith.

Addington, Oklahoma, is named for Zach and his brother and cousin: **Columbus (C.C.) Addington** (April 18, 1850–November 28, 1894—buried November 10, 1896) and **Andrew J. "Andy" Addington** (July 28,1850–December 19, 1938). (MAP: ZA)

First Wife of Founder of Marietta, Indian Territory

This once magnificent, ornate monument that has a headless, wingless angel leaning against it in the Addington family plot was a symbol of the esteem Jeremiah "Jerry" Calvin Washington had for his first (of three) wives, **Josie Addington Washington** (May 8, 1860–November 25, 1882), and a

This fallen, headless angel marks the grave of Josie Washington, wife of the founder of Marietta, Indian Territory.

reflection of his wealth. Next to Josie is a small ornate monument marking the grave of a son, **Jarrett R. Washington** (October 6, 1879–April 23, 1882), who preceded his mother in death and was apparently named for his grandfather, **Jarrett Addington** (May 29, 1817–July 3, 1891).

Jerry Washington was born on July 3, 1857, in Cooke County, son of James Russell Washington Sr. and Sallie Jones Washington. His father had ranching operations in Cooke County and expanded operations into Indian Territory about 1868. Jerry and his brother W.E. "Colonel Billy" became two of the largest landholders in Indian Territory in Pickens County, which became Love County. Jerry's half sister, Rosa McLish, was married to the founder of Ardmore, Richard McLish.

Jerry became the first postmaster of Marietta and was a predominant landowner and banker in that city. He was generous in giving away town lots to churches and widows, similar to J.M. Lindsay in Gainesville. The origin of the name of the town "Marietta" is disputed. One version has Marietta named for Marietta, Pennsylvania, by the Gulf, Colorado and Santa Fe Railroad when it established its station in the middle of Washington's landholdings. The other version is that Marietta is named for Jerry's second wife, Marietta Mae "Mamie" Bell Love. (MAP: JW)

UNION VETERAN

Jacob Beckelman (June 24, 1837–July 1, 1913) is the only member of the Grand Army of the Republic (GAR) identified as such in Fairview. The GAR was the Union veterans' organization that coexisted with the ex-Confederate organization. Beckelman belonged to GAR Samuel R. Curtis Post #12 in Gainesville. Bonham, Whitesboro and Denton were the only other Texas cities with GAR posts.

Beckelman's tombstone shared with his wife, **Margarette** (August 20, 1849–March 4, 1920), declares: "God's Finger Touched Him and He Slept." (MAP: JB)

"MYSTERY MAN'S" ORNATE WOODMEN OF THE WORLD MONUMENT

Many Woodmen of the World monuments dot the landscape of Fairview, but the Woodmen monument of **Elias Rahal Simon** (December 4 or December 22, 1887–December 24, 1909 or January 6, 1910) is the most ornate. Simon's conflicting birth and death dates are due to the different dates on the monument, one inscription in English and one in Lebanese. Despite his porcelain portrait on his marker, this young man is a "mystery man." It is remarkable that his portrait is in pristine condition after almost one hundred years. The button on his suit is probably a Woodmen button. This eternally young man emigrated from Jdaidat Marjaayoun, a village in Lebanon, according to the foreign language inscription at the base of the monument.

The Woodmen of the World Life Insurance Society was founded on June 4, 1890, by Joseph Cullen Root in Omaha, Nebraska. According to *The*

Woodmen Story: Our First 100 Years, Root "recognized the analogy—that as woodsmen clear forests to build shelters for their families, members would shelter their families with life insurance and fraternal protection." The tree stump is the symbol of Woodmen, symbolizing a life cut short. The axe and the maul that commonly adorn Woodmen monuments are tools of the woodsman. The Woodmen organization was committed to mark all graves of its members, regardless of their ability to pay.

Woodmen Circle was established for female members and for men who wanted more than the $3,000 limit on insurance. The objectives of "Woodcraft [are] to ennoble its membership; to minister to the afflicted; to relieve distress; to seek employment for those without it; to cast a sheltering arm about the defenseless living; to give honorable burial to our sacred dead." From 1930 to 1972, Woodmen Circle maintained a Home for Orphans and Aged Members in nearby Sherman. (MAP: ES)

Infant of Famous Spur Maker

Identified only as "Infant of **McChesney**," this is probably the infant of J.R. and Tabitha McChesney, who lived in Gainesville from about 1890 to 1910. The McChesney family moved here from Broken Arrow, Oklahoma. By trade, J.R. was originally a blacksmith, but he opened a blacksmith shop combined with bicycle repair shop and ultimately manufactured spurs and bits. His first shop was in a retired trolley car, and then he moved his shop to the corner of Olive and Taylor Streets. He was the "Father of the (one-piece) Texas spur," according to Lee C. Jacobs, author of *J.R. McChesney: A Lifetime, a Legacy*. He moved his well-renowned spur-making establishment from here to Pauls Valley, Oklahoma. (MAP: IM)

Mayor and Babysitter

George Y. (Yell) Bird (November 16, 1829–November 4, 1906) was a prominent merchant whose business was on the southwest corner of the courthouse square. His store was in the first brick building in Gainesville. Bird would sometimes babysit children of customers when they frequented a less safe part of town.

This is the portrait of early Gainesville mayor George Y. Bird, who babysat the children of the customers of his general store while they went to the rougher part of town. *Courtesy of Morton Museum of Cooke County.*

He was mayor of Gainesville under a new charter in 1873. Bird, **J.M. Lindsay** (Division 8) and **F.M. Dougherty** (Division 19) planned the county's first poor farm in 1876. He and his wife, **Elizabeth M. Bird** (February 1, 1840–November 27, 1887), have tombstones of a scroll design next to the street on the west side of Division 4. (MAP: GB)

FIRST COOKE COUNTY HOME DEMONSTRATION AGENT

Berlie Bolton Ross (November 5, 1886–April 4, 1964) was Miss Berlie Bolton when she came to Gainesville in 1922 after Mildred Horton of the Texas A&M Extension Service convinced county judge H.S. Holman and the county commissioners of the need of a county home demonstration agent. Miss Bolton came here from the faculty of North Texas Agricultural College of Arlington.

From a nucleus of 4-H Boys Clubs that already existed, she organized 4-H Girls Clubs at Era, Valley View, Marysville, Bulcher, Sivells Bend, Callisburg, Woodbine, Vilott, Myra and Lindsay shortly after her arrival. Berlie Bolton also organized the first women's home demonstration club in the Reed community; the group was called the Bolton Home Demonstration Club. Subsequent clubs were organized at Freemound, Rosston, Lois, Whaley Chapel, Dexter and Spring Creek.

Miss Bolton's success was responsible for her brief career as home demonstration agent. Evidently, her impressive "Rural Relations" dinner caught the attention of her future husband, **Ancil Henry Ross** (April 14, 1877–June 21, 1956). That dinner in August 1923 was sponsored by the Rotary Club and was held on the second floor of Ross Brothers Hardware, owned by Ancil and J.W. "Will" Ross. Less than one year later, Ancil and Berlie were married on June 18, 1924.

Ancil Ross was a civic leader of Gainesville. He had a varied business career, including hardware, automobiles and two years as county auditor. Ross was former president of the Rotary Club and the Gainesville Chamber of Commerce, former grandmaster of the Masonic lodge and member of the board of stewards of First Methodist Church. (MAP: BR)

Pioneer of Gainesville Theatre

Paul Gallia (1854–October 10, 1934) came to Gainesville with his bride, **Betty Rudolph Gallia** (1864–March 19, 1941) of McKinney, to manage an opera house for **Joe Means** (Division 15), the owner of the *Gainesville Hesperian*. Gallia's first two opera houses were on the second floor of downtown buildings.

In 1895, Gallia successfully raised $4,000 and, with **Harvey Hulen** (Division 6) as his partner, razed the brick mansion of **Zach Addington** (Division 4) and moved the dismantled building to Rusk and Main Streets to be recycled into the impressive three-story Gallia Opera House. It attracted many notable performers in its heyday, including the band of John Philip Sousa. In 1928, with Gallia on the Knights of Pythias building committee, that fraternal order converted the opera house to the Pythian Castle Hall.

There was a special Knights of Pythias edition of the *Gainesville Register* celebrating that event.

In 1887, the City of Gainesville hired Gallia to paint house numbers on Gainesville's houses. From 1901 to 1903, he was business manager for the short-lived *Daily Messenger*, which was owned by his brother-in-law, J.K. Rudolph. Later in life, Gallia operated a sign-painting and poster business. (MAP: GA)

"PRINCESS OF GAINESVILLE"

The death of ten-year-old **Nannie Pauline "Tincie" Gallia** (b. Oct. 3, 1885), daughter of **Paul** and **Betty Gallia**, on Christmas morning 1895 elicited citywide mourning. In an age when deaths of children were not

This Italian marble bust used to grace the grave of ten-year-old Tincie Gallia. It was stolen from the grave approximately ten years ago.

uncommon, the *Hesperian* devoted an unusual amount of space to eulogizing the young girl:

> *While the world was waking to the joyous Christmas festivities, little Tincie Gallia gave up the struggle for life, and yielded back the sweet spirit that had been lent awhile to make earth less sad.*
>
> *Perhaps the angels that came to sing, "peace on earth and good will to man," bore home with them, the tender bud that for a season shed such sweet fragrance around the hearth and social circle, and gave such promise of future perfection.*
>
> *Tincie was called away before her little feet had learned the paths of sins, or her tender heart had felt the bruises or disappointments that come to all grown up children.*

Tincie's grave site has features of a Victorian-age, well-marked small child's grave. Marble stone makes the outline of a cradle. The pedestal of the missing Italian marble bust features the words "Our Treasure." (MAP: GA)

Pioneer in Hardware

Frank L. Cleaves (1830–July 10, 1901), native of Vermont, at the age of nineteen was one of those thousands of Forty-Niners who went to the California gold fields. In 1858, he paid for stagecoach fare from Sacramento to Gainesville with gold dust. In 1860, he married sixteen-year-old **Dallas Latimer** (1844–May 30, 1930), who had also come to Gainesville in 1858 as a boarding school student from Grayson County.

Cleaves was a tax collection official for a four-county area for several years prior to forming the Cleaves & (Henry B.) Fletcher Hardware partnership about 1875. Their hardware store occupied the block surrounded by South Dixon, California, Rusk and Bogg (now Main) Streets, just east of the courthouse.

Henry B. Sanborn, future founder of Amarillo, made history by coming into Cleaves's store in September 1875 after a long train ride from Illinois to Denison and a buggy ride from Denison. He sold Cleaves and Fletcher ten reels of "Glidden Number 5" barbed wire he had brought from Illinois. This was the first sale of this newly patented, two-stranded barbed wire in Texas. (MAP: FC)

U.S. DEPUTY MARSHAL KILLED IN SHOOTOUT IN INDIAN TERRITORY

Edgar A. Stokley (1860–December 3, 1887), U.S. deputy marshal, was shot to death while attempting to arrest twenty-year-old Will Towerly, a young horse thief and murderer, at his folks' home on Boggy Creek near Atoka, Indian Territory. Stokley was part of a posse attempting to arrest Towerly, who had killed U.S. Deputy Marshal Frank Dalton a week earlier. (Frank, a respected deputy, was the oldest brother of a group of brothers who would later become the "Dalton gang.")

Deputy Stokley's undoing was simply trying to shoot a cold-blooded killer with the idea of disarming him rather than killing him. Deputy Z.W. "Bill" Moody had shot Towerly in the shoulder and in the leg. Towerly was able to switch his gun from his wounded arm to the other and fatally shoot Stokley twice as he approached him. Young Towerly's mother and sister interfered with Deputy Moody during the shootout. They clawed his hands and pushed him through the front door into the house during the shooting. Moody continued his firing through a window of the house and was able to fatally wound Towerly, saving him from the hangman's noose at Fort Smith. Moody survived this episode only to be killed a short time later by outlaw Billy Bruner.

According to Ron Owens in *Oklahoma Heroes*, Stokley had worked in law enforcement in the Chickasaw Nation for approximately one year. The famous U.S. marshal Heck Thomas had recommended Stokley for his appointment as deputy marshal. Stokley was the fifteenth U.S. marshal to be killed in Indian Territory in two years. The deputy lived with his father near Marietta, Indian Territory. According to *Oklahoma Outlaws Lawmen History Association Online*, Stokley was planning to marry Josie Peterman of Callisburg on January 25, 1888. The deputy's body was shipped by Katy train to Gainesville and received at the home of **Harvey Hulen** (Division 6) until the funeral the following day. At this date, Deputy Stokley has an unmarked grave. (MAP: ST)

Moral of the Story: If Bitten by Suspicious Animal, Consult a Doctor Immediately

Six-year-old **Mary Altie Rushing** (December 31, 1909–January 31, 1916) died from being bitten on the hand by a strange, rabid puppy that had been hanging around her house near the Gainesville brick plant. She died two days after being bitten. Perhaps Altie thought the bite was trivial and didn't tell her parents until it was too late. When doctors were contacted, she was already experiencing the rigors that usually precede death.

If her parents had known of her condition soon after she was bitten, they might have located someone with a mad stone and possibly cured her. A mad stone was a common cure for rabies and other poisonous bites before vaccine was developed. There were a number of cases of people in the Gainesville area cured by the mad stone treatment. A mad stone was a kind of hairball from the stomach of a cow or deer. Soaked in warm milk and held against a fresh bite, it would stick to the wound if it were poisonous and fall off after it had done its job of sucking out the poison. The tradition was that if you possessed a mad stone, you could not charge for treating someone and you could not sell the stone.

Mary Altie's mother, **Ida Nee Canady Rushing** (December 25, 1872–February 20, 1971), is buried next to her. (MAP: AR)

Justice of the Peace, Local Historian

C.N. (Charles Nelson) Jones (March 18, 1858–March 22, 1942), Gainesville pioneer, had a long and diverse life. He was a cowboy, a farmer, a justice of the peace, a preacher and in his retired years worked to preserve local history.

Jones was born in Buncombe County, North Carolina, the son of Sarah Neilson and Richard Manson Jones. From the age of two through five, he lived on Clear Creek near the community of Leo in southwest Cooke County. During the Civil War, his mother moved the family to Fannin County to live with her parents while her husband fought as a volunteer in Company C of the Texas Volunteer Infantry for the Confederacy. He was killed in fighting at Calcasieu Pass, Louisiana, in 1864.

Shortly after Charley's mother married Colonel A.B. Manion of Delaware Bend, Charley and his brother moved to Mrs. Underwood's boardinghouse in Gainesville to attend school conducted by Reverend E.W. Alderson, a Methodist minister. Later, as a longtime member of Whaley Methodist Church, Jones would preach at a number of Cooke County churches and serve as a "supply pastor" for two years at Bells and Petty.

As a young man, he helped haul lumber to build the first frame house in Gainesville, according to the *Register.* He spent two years working as a cowboy in West Texas and then returned to Gainesville for similar work. In 1879, he married **Sarah Elizabeth "Bettie" Boyd** of the Clear Creek community. They farmed the old homeplace near Leo until 1892, when they moved to Gainesville to take advantage of the schools for their five children. (Eventually, they would have ten children.)

Jones's first job in Gainesville after permanently moving here was as janitor of the new high school on the corner of Denton and Scott Streets. He served as a justice of the peace in the courthouse from 1931 to 1938. Aided by contributions from the local United Daughters of the Confederacy, he maintained a significant collection of Civil War artifacts, including guns, swords and other articles on display in a room of the courthouse.

However, after his retirement, the collection was moved to a log cabin in Fair Park. That building later burned along with that Civil War collection, according to his granddaughter, **Margaret Parx Hays** (Division 24), who wrote the foreword to C.N. Jones's *Early Days in Cooke County, 1858–1873.* (MAP: CJ)

GLAMOROUS TEXAS RANGER

Captain Tom (Thomas Rufus) Hickman (February 21, 1886–January 29, 1962), a famous and colorful Texas Ranger who is featured in the Texas Ranger Hall of Fame and Museum in Waco, is buried between two wives: **Mayme K. Hickman** (August 4, 1895–April 18, 1924) and **Tina Martha (Knight) Hickman** (January 29, 1905–December 26, 1979).

When Tom was born in the Marysville area of northwestern Cooke County, his parents, Walter B. and Mary McCormick Hickman, had no name for their new baby until they were inspired by a visit of a white man named Tom and an Indian named Rufus. Tom grew up around guns and

Tom Hickman, Texas Ranger, actor and rodeo judge, is also a featured attraction at the Texas Ranger Hall of Fame and Museum in Waco. He is buried here between two wives. *Courtesy of Morton Museum of Cooke County.*

horses. He attended Gainesville High School and Gainesville Business College. He played football when they played without pads. Tom's first venture in the area of law enforcement was as fire marshal and deputy constable in Gainesville.

In 1919, Tom Hickman was appointed a Texas Ranger by Governor William Hobby. His work involved the Texas-Oklahoma border dispute and maintaining law and order in the rough oil boomtowns of Borger, Eastland, Cisco and Mexia. According to the *Register*, he shot two bank robbers with one shot in the act of robbing a bank in Clarksville. Captain Hickman developed a habit of taking care of the Rangers under his command by renting a large house for all of them when on an assignment and providing them with a cook.

He retired from the Texas Rangers in 1935 and did security work for Gulf Oil Company after his retirement. In 1956, he was appointed to the Texas Public Safety Commission, which has supervisory power over the Texas Rangers and Texas Highway Patrol.

Tom Hickman had a reputation that went beyond his law enforcement experiences. He was a friend of Tom Mix and Will Rogers. Hickman was in numerous plays in the local theatre. In 1929, he played a Texas Ranger in the Little Theatre production of *The Bad Man*, which was inspired by the exploits of Pancho Villa. Hickman also did demonstration marksmanship for the Gainesville Community Circus.

He was a regular at leading local parades on horseback, although in recent times the trend is for horseback riders to be at the end of parades for practical sanitation reasons. Former Gainesville Texas Ranger **Lewis Rigler** (Division 9) recalled in *In the Line of Duty* the story about Tom being grand marshal of the Gainesville Community Circus parade in 1951. Tom was posing on horseback for photographers before the parade started. The reporter for the *Fort Worth Star-Telegram*, who was trying to take pictures, whispered to Rigler, who was standing beside him, that he was out of film. Lewis Rigler's reply was, "Keep on snapping and make him happy."

Tom Hickman also had a national and international reputation as a rodeo judge. He served as rodeo judge in Boston, Detroit, Chicago, New York and London. In 1930, he toured Europe with the Simmons (Hardin-Simmons) University Band. In 1957, to celebrate the fiftieth anniversary of the Southwestern Fat Stock Show and Exposition, he braved a winter storm to ride by horseback 125 miles of the Chisholm Trail to Fort Worth. From *In the Line of Duty*: "Women waved at me, dogs barked at me, and men laughed at me."

After having surgery for prostate cancer in Dallas in the fall of 1961, he refused further hospitalization and died at his home south of Gainesville on January 29, 1962. Lewis Rigler was with him when he died.

Mayme (August 4, 1895–April 18, 1924), Tom's first wife, died tragically in 1924. While she and Tom were packing for a trip to Europe, the short-barreled rifle she was packing discharged, killing her instantly.

Tom's second wife, **Tina** (January 29, 1905–December 26, 1979), was eighteen years younger than her husband. In fact, she and her family lived on Hickman land. You might say he literally "robbed the cradle," because he had rocked her to sleep when she was a baby. He had two sons from his marriage with Tina: David and Tom Jr. "Dogie." (MAP: TH)

Renounced Allegiance to the King of Sweden

(Charles) C.J. Johnson died at the age of seventy-six and was buried on January 14, 1932. He is representative of the foreign-born who came to Cooke County for a better life. According to a Declaration of Intention (to become a United States citizen) filed with the district court, he was born in Yetada, Sweden, on April 16, 1855. He emigrated from Gnennock, Scotland, in 1879 via the port of Pensacola, Florida. In his Declaration of Intention, which he signed on January 4, 1924, he renounced his allegiance to the King of Sweden and swore he was neither an anarchist nor a polygamist.

According to his personal description in 1924, he was five feet, nine inches tall, weighed 135 pounds, had gray hair and light blue eyes and a tattoo on each arm. He was a plumber by trade. His wife, **Edla Matilda**, also residing at 415 Hall Street, was also born in Sweden. She was buried on November 18, 1940. (MAP: JO)

Former President of the Fairview Cemetery Association

Tennie Bonner Lindsay (December 10, 1846–March 7, 1922) was the wife of **J.M. Lindsay** (Division 8). She was born in Paris, Texas, the daughter of **George M.** (July 20, 1812–April 7, 1864) and **Elizabeth D. Bonner** (September 19, 1817–March 11, 1899), who are both buried in Division 4. Tennie was fourteen years old when her family moved from Lamar County and settled south of the town of Lindsay. She married J.M. Lindsay when she was twenty-five years old. Their two children—son **Lewis B. Lindsay** (August 31, 1871–May 13, 1934) and daughter **Jimmie T. Embrey** (December 4, 1877–January 2, 1933)—are buried near their father. Tennie is in the Bonner family plot.

Tennie Lindsay was a civic-minded Christian lady whose civic activities won her many admirers. In addition to promoting the beautification of Fairview as president of the cemetery association, she was instrumental in promoting the Orphans Home in its early years. Any civic organization—and there were numerous ones—received a boost when she was involved. She was a longtime active member of Denton Street Methodist Church. Tennie Street in Gainesville is named for her. (MAP: TL)

THROWN FROM A HORSE

Harold Cairns Potter (September 23, 1884–June 29, 1895), the ten-year-old son of former district judge **Clement Clay Potter** (August 30, 1847–March 28, 1918) and **Zella Bogardus Potter** (February 19, 1853–September 27, 1918), died after being thrown from a horse. His funeral was held at his home at 33 Church Street. (MAP: HP)

LONGTIME LEGISLATOR

Jesse C. Murrell (May 12, 1856–November 14, 1927) was born in Ray County, Missouri. His great-grandfather was Colonel Samuel Murrell, a Virginia officer in the Revolutionary War. His ancestors on both sides of the family were wealthy planters and slaveholders.

Jesse's family moved to the Walnut Bend area in 1860 after several years in Fannin County. After his education in Cooke County schools, Murrell was both a merchant and a farmer, finally settling on being a farmer. On July 20, 1893, he married **Ada J. Moss** (1859–unknown) of Gainesville.

Murrell became involved in Democratic Party politics as a young adult, consistently attending county and state conventions. He was elected three consecutive terms to the Texas House of Representatives, from 1889 to 1893, easily defeating his Populist opponent. He then returned for two terms in 1901 and 1903 and later in 1917 and 1919. In both the 1891 and 1893 sessions of the legislature, he introduced bills to punish those who tore down a fence or left a gate open that let livestock out. He was also the author of the constitutional amendment that provided for a poll tax. Murrell did not approve of the state's method of having uniform adoption of textbooks, which he believed resulted in textbook companies' "extortion of the people's money."

Murrell died suddenly in Dorchester, Texas. He was a member of First Methodist Church and of the Gainesville Masonic Lodge #210. E.V. Cole, former minister of First Methodist and editor of the *Texas Christian Advocate*, presided over his funeral. (MAP: MU)

The "Santa Claus" Engineer

Joseph Michael Gerard (February 13, 1867–May 27, 1947) had the most tenure as an employee of the Santa Fe Railroad, fifty-seven years, when he retired in 1942. He fittingly died in the Santa Fe hospital in Temple.

He started his railroad career for Santa Fe in Goldthwaite, Texas, in 1885 and joined his brother, **Ernest Gerard** (November 19, 1861–July 19, 1903), in Gainesville in 1886. His brother piloted the first Santa Fe locomotive into Gainesville that year over the Katy tracks, since the Santa Fe tracks had not been laid yet.

For most of his years in Gainesville, Joe piloted the passenger train from here to Purcell, Oklahoma, until he was transferred to Cleburne in 1901. The rest of his career, he was passenger engineer from Cleburne via Gainesville to Purcell.

Joe developed a national reputation as the "Santa Claus" engineer because of his habit of throwing Christmas presents from the cab of his locomotive to "destitute families who lived in dugouts, huts or cabins adjacent to the right-of-way." According to the *Register*, he also threw out magazines and newspapers to those same people. Joe Gerard was their connection to the outside world. One young woman claimed that latter service of his was the basis of her education. (MAP: JG)

Her Living Legacy

If any gravestone is understated, it is that of **Mary Josephine Cox** (1854?–September 8, 1934). It simply has her name.

When Miss Cox failed to show up on the first day of school in the fall of 1934, she was found dead in her apartment in "the Flats" on the corner of Denton and Main Streets. Approximately eighty years old, she had taught English in the Gainesville public school system and at Gainesville Junior College for forty-two years.

Miss Cox accumulated an impressive number of books, and she read regularly to **R.J. Timmis Sr.** (Division 15), who was blind as a result of his harrowing experience as a passenger on the ill-fated *Lusitania.*

This double exposure of the face of Mary Josephine Cox over her tombstone won the Humanities Class Photography Contest at North Central Texas College in the spring of 1997. *With permission of photographer Twila Farrar.*

She walked everywhere in tennis shoes, and her students created a park on school grounds in her honor because of her love of the outdoors. She bequeathed in her will several parcels of land to create a scholarship fund for boys and girls of Cooke County to attend the local college. In 1945, two oil wells were successfully drilled on her estate, and they have produced revenue for hundreds of scholarships. That fund continues to be healthy.

The "300 Building" on the North Central Texas College campus in Gainesville bears her name. It initially housed the college library, but today it is a nursing classroom–administrative building. (MAP: MC)

Division 5

Bertillion Expert Died of Apparent Heart Attack

Cecil J. Burch (April 3, 1888–April 5, 1933), a longtime local law enforcement officer, died unexpectedly of an apparent heart attack in his sleep while staying with his wife in a Mineral Wells hotel. According to the *Register*, Burch probably had the most tenure as a police officer in the county.

As a young man, he turned his interest in fingerprinting (bertillion science) into a career in law enforcement. He served in that field as policeman, deputy sheriff, county detective and, finally, fingerprinting expert. His skill in fingerprinting put him in big demand in this area, especially solving burglaries. His picture is among a collection of pictures of officials on the wall in the Cooke County Courthouse. (MAP: CB)

Division 6

Pioneer Livestock Owner, Public Servant and Businessman

Harvey H. Hulen (1845–October 1932) was born in Missouri, and he and his wife, **France May "Fannie" May Morter** (1849–September 1936), came to Cooke County from Boone County, Missouri, in 1873. Hulen and several others met in Valley View in 1875 to organize a cattlemen's organization to stop cattle rustling in the area. This was the forerunner of the Southwestern Cattlemen's Association. In 1891, Hulen's Berkshire hogs were prizewinners at the county fair held a short distance away from this cemetery at Fair Street and Broadway.

He was elected two terms as county surveyor beginning in 1876 and elected one term as county tax collector in 1880. He later served two terms as a Gainesville city councilman. In 1893, he became a charter member of Melita Commandery No. 30 of the Knights Templar of Gainesville and was eminent commander of that chapter from 1893 to 1895. Also in 1895, he was partner with **Paul Gallia** (Division 4) in building the Gainesville Opera House. (MAP: HU)

Rookie Texas Ranger Killed in His First Gun Battle

Eugene "Gene" B. Hulen (1876–June 1915), son of **Harvey H.** and **Fannie M. Hulen**, had no experience in law enforcement but received his commission as a Texas Ranger on March 29, 1915, primarily because of the influence of his brother, John A. Hulen. This was in a period when the Texas Rangers were especially susceptible to political influences during the administration of Governor James "Pa" Ferguson. John Hulen was an influential railroad executive and former adjunct general of the Texas National Guard at the time of his brother's appointment.

Scarcely three months after his appointment, Ranger Gene Hulen was killed along with former Ranger and customs inspector Joe Sitter in an ambush led by Mexican bandit Chico Cano in the Big Bend area. Three Texas Rangers were near Hulen and Sitter when they were ambushed but did not come to their rescue. An eleven-man posse from Marfa located the bodies of Hulen and Sitter the next day. Evidence suggested that Hulen died early in the gun battle. After being shot numerous times, Hulen and Sitter had been stripped naked and beaten in the face to the point of being unrecognizable. The stench of the decaying bodies caused one of the mules carrying the bodies from the ambush site to vomit. Harris and Sadler's account of this in *The Texas Rangers and the Mexican Revolution* erroneously suggests that Hulen was buried in Houston.

Hulen, an 1893 graduate of Gainesville High School, prophetically read his graduate essay entitled "Moral Courage" at his commencement ceremony. (MAP: HU)

Division 7

East of 6 and 6A

His Family Received One of the Last 320-Acre Land Patents in the County

J.M. (John) Estes (August 13, 1849–March 11, 1928) was born in Hickman County, Tennessee, and came to Texas with his parents as a three-year-old. After one year in Smith County, they settled in Cooke County on Clear Creek near Rosston. Estes's family was one of the last families to claim 320 acres of land from the state thirteen days before the Pre-Emption Act of 1853 expired.

At the time their house was built, there was only one other in addition to theirs located between Gainesville and Fort Belknap, a distance today of 116 miles. Back then that distance was a three-day trip by horseback. The last Indian raid in Cooke County, which resulted in the death of one woman and four children, occurred near their dwelling in 1868. As a boy, Estes saw threatening Indians but, fortunately, not up close.

After Estes retired and moved to Gainesville, he became one of the founding members of the Half Century Club, a club for those who had lived in Cooke County at least half a century. (MAP: JE)

A Meticulous Suicide

Henry Bier (March 20, 1868–May 15, 1931), longtime merchant and owner of Gainesville Brick Company, shot himself fatally in the chest in a northeast room of his former residence on Church Street. He had been despondent over recent "business reverses" and the death of his son, **Edwin** (May 10, 1905–April 21, 1929), manager of his brick company in Gainesville, who died suddenly of a cerebral hemorrhage. Henry's mother, **"Madame" Laura Bier** (September 16, 1842–February 22, 1928), an emigrant from France who owned a dry goods store in Gainesville for many years, had also died the previous year.

Bier had entered the business world as a partner of his mother in the dry goods business. Then, in the early 1900s, he bought the New Odorless Sewerage Company from its original owners and operated it until the City of Gainesville purchased it in 1921. He closed his brick plant shortly after the death of his son and moved to Dallas, where he acquired the Plaza Pharmacy in University Heights and some residential properties.

Because of frequent business trips back to Gainesville from Dallas, Bier had arranged to reserve a room in his former residence, which he had rented out. Shortly before Bier committed suicide, he telephoned J.D. Howeth to summon him to his room. He apparently spent most of the morning writing a half-dozen farewells to his wife, family and friends and had meticulously labeled keys to various properties he owned. Bier requested that the Knights of Pythias, in which he was a member, act as pallbearers at his funeral, which he requested to be brief.

On the table in his room was a picture of his son, Edwin, and a Bible opened to John 17:23–18:23, which describes Judas's betrayal and Peter's first denial of Christ. (MAP:BI)

Gainesville's "Cinderella"

Although **Augusta Bier** (September 24, 1876–February 10, 1973) moved to Gainesville about 1896 as the bride of **Henry Bier** (March 20, 1868–May 15, 1931), she had been a New Orleans celebrity shortly before her marriage.

She became part of a national obsession in the United States with George du Maurier's novel, *Trilby*, published in 1894 and subsequently made into

On the left is Augusta Ferrandou when she won the *Trilby* shoe competition in New Orleans in the 1890s; on the right is Augusta Bier in 1931. *Taken from* Gainesville Register *microfilm, Cooke County Library.*

a play. A leading character in the novel is Trilby, an untalented Parisian artist model who is transformed into a singing sensation in mid-nineteenth-century Europe by being hypnotized by the villainous Svengali.

A number of items associated with the novel and play were mass produced, including a Trilby hat and Trilby shoes. The character, Trilby, had a "perfect foot" that was sketched on the wall in the scene of the play depicting the artist's studio. Ice cream was sold in the shape of the "Trilby foot." Macon, Florida, was renamed Trilby.

At the time of this frenzy, Augusta (then Miss Ferrandou), although of French ancestry, was the daughter of the Colombian consul in New Orleans. She had recently completed her studies at a local convent school when she and her sister noticed a pair of diminutive Trilby slippers displayed in a Canal Street storefront. The shoes were advertising a contest for the appropriate lady whose feet fit the shoes to win the shoes, to be awarded at a performance of *Trilby* at the New Orleans Academy of Music.

Augusta was a finalist with two other young ladies who were judged by two shoe experts who had come from Massachusetts and New York. Her two competitors had to have the top strap of the shoe stretched with a buttonhook. Augusta won since she could button the shoe with her bare hand. "Cinderella's" father forbade her to receive the shoes on the stage of the performance from the cast, so the theatre manager presented them to her as she stood in the audience between acts of the play.

Much of this personal story appeared in a *Gainesville Register* article that was prompted by the showing of the talking picture *Svengali* in Dallas in July 1931, a couple of months after Augusta's husband's suicide.

Augusta Bier was a resident of Dallas at the time and taught French privately in her home. She admitted that the only things left of the shoes were the buckles. Her three daughters had worn out the shoes playing in them. (MAP: BI)

Outlaw "Black Sheep" of the Family

Haney Horace Hix Liddell (June 15, 1893–November 21, 1928) died from wounds he received about one week after robbing the First National Bank of Marietta, Oklahoma. Until being shot during his second bank robbery, Liddell had eluded law enforcement officers for almost ten months after his robbery of the Love County National Bank in Marietta on January 25, 1928. In that robbery, Love County Sheriff Sam C. Long was mortally wounded, and Liddell's accomplice, Oscar Harrison was killed.

At the time of his second bank robbery, Liddell had a disguise of a dark beard and fake red mustache. He was wearing homemade body armor made out of Ford transmission cases that protected his torso. However, he was superficially wounded in one leg and both arms. Infection from shotgun pellets, which blinded him in both eyes, was what proved fatal. He was probably wounded in trying to retrieve his accomplice, Colbert Keel, who fell out of their getaway Ford during a running gun battle.

Gainesville newspaper publisher **Joe M. Leonard Sr.** (Division K) interviewed Liddell in his jail cell shortly before he died. (Haney had a wife and three-year-old child.) His only explanation for his career in crime was that when he started "going bad" he just could not stop. Back in 1917, Liddell was accused of shooting to death **Tom M. Boyd**, a Thackerville tenant farmer with six children. Liddell was convicted of manslaughter in that case but "got off" on appeal. Boyd is buried next to his sister, **Ida Tippit** (Division 22).

This account is drawn from Joe M. Leonard Jr.'s *Bah Bah Black Sheep*. The title of this book is a reference to other family members, notably Liddell's two sisters, **Martha** and **Voncille Liddell**, who had distinguished careers teaching in Gainesville High School and Gainesville Junior College. They are buried together in the family plot. (MAP: HL)

Death from One Bite of an Apple

Kenneth M. Hall (1911–November 25, 1928), a seventeen-year-old freshman at the University of Texas, according to the *Register*, accidentally poisoned himself by putting potassium cyanide crystals on an apple instead of salt. He died in his dorm room after eating one bite of the apple.

According to the newspaper article, he and some friends bought some apples and returned to their rooms after attending a movie. Hall was a diligent chemistry student, although he planned to make a career in law. He took the cyanide from the chemistry lab to do some experiments in his room. The cyanide was in a container identical to a saltshaker, and the assumption was that he picked it up instead of the saltshaker.

According to the *Register*, he was an "exceptional student" at Newsome Dougherty Memorial High School, where he excelled in debate. "His teachers and friends had foreseen for him a brilliant future…and he was making splendid progress at the University when his untimely death occurred."

Kenneth is buried with his father and mother, **Moss** and **Margaret Hall**. (MAP: KH)

Downtown Shootout Claims the Life of Fire Marshal and Patrolman

J. Walter Clements (January 1, 1888–July 24, 1931), Gainesville fire marshal, was shotgunned to death by **Frank M. Bracken** (Division 21) as he stepped from his Ford coupe parked on California Street in front of W.W. Howeth Abstract Company. Gainesville motorcycle patrolman William E. Johns was also mortally wounded by Bracken. Another motorcycle officer, Charles Tune, wounded Bracken in the wrist before he was apprehended.

More than a dozen shots were fired, some shattering plate-glass windows and some riddling cars.

According to the first account of the shootout in the *Register*, Johns had trouble returning fire at Bracken because his gun wasn't loaded. A later explanation was that Johns was reluctant to shoot Bracken because they had been buddies in the army. Johns died a little over a week after the shooting. He is buried in Valley View.

Clements's first wife was the former Gertrude Hogan of Callisburg. She died in 1912, and Clements married the former Alice Harris in 1915. Clements had been fire marshal for approximately three months. Prior to that he had been in the moving business and then the automobile business. (MAP: WC)

Gainesville Police Chief Shot to Death Former Patrolman

Mitchell Alvin Truitt (January 27, 1911–March 27, 1942) was shot and killed in the barnyard of his home in Woodbine by his former boss, Gainesville Police Chief Harvey Olmon. According to one who viewed his body, Truitt was shot thirteen times. A witness at the scene said the assailant fled the scene with a woman in the car.

Olmon voluntarily surrendered to Sheriff Carl Wilson at the courthouse the following morning, also turning over his .38 automatic pistol. He was charged with "murder with malice aforethought."

Truitt married Mrs. Rhoda Fitzgerald in 1938. He left the Gainesville Police Department in December 1941 after purchasing a farm in Woodbine, financed by the Farm Security Administration. Sheriff Wilson was one of the pallbearers at Truitt's funeral, which produced a large turnout at Commerce Street Church of Christ.

On a change of venue, Olmon was tried for murder in the Fifty-ninth District Court in Sherman in December 1942. After twenty-four hours of deliberation, the jury acquitted Olmon based on his claim of self-defense. Olmon got into an argument with Truitt concerning Truitt's debt problems, and the police chief believed Truitt was going for a gun Olmon thought Truitt had in his front pants pocket.

Mitchell Truitt's son, **Maurice Truitt** (1939–1983), is buried next to his father. His marker identifies him as "A3C U.S. Air Force." (MAP: MT)

President of the "Hooters"

Dr. William Herbert Locke (May 20, 1895–October 6, 1971), who served as a sergeant in the Kansas Medical Department during World War I, was an osteopathic doctor who practiced medicine for over three decades in Gainesville. However, many people knew him as a promoter of softball and professional baseball in Gainesville.

Three owners acquired a Class B professional baseball team for Gainesville, the Gainesville Owls, in 1947. In their seven and a half years of existence here, the *Gainesville Register* habitually referred to the team as the "Hooters." Financial difficulties led a large group of citizens to raise $35,000 to keep the team here. They made Dr. Locke their president, and the baseball field with its covered grandstand became Locke Field. From 1947 to 1951, Gainesville was a member of the Big State League and was the smallest city in the United States to have a Class B baseball franchise. The Hooters were league champion in 1951.

The team had a hiatus in 1952 but came back and survived as a Class D franchise as part of the Sooner State League from 1953 until May 19, 1955, as a farm team for the Chicago Cubs. Toward the end, games averaged 150 in attendance, and the league abruptly converted the Hooters to the Ponca City Jets in the middle of the season. Sportswriter Bill King blamed the team's demise on a losing season and competition with television.

Coincidentally, Dr. Locke also left Gainesville the same year the baseball team left. He moved to Grand Prairie. The City of Gainesville is the owner of Locke Field, but the future of the historic baseball field is in doubt. In recent years, the city had an agreement with Gainesville Independent School District, which used the field for high school games. Voters in May 2010 voted to allow the city to lease the property but voted down the proposal to sell it. Locke Field is the only one of four previously existing covered grandstands in the Sooner State League. Those in Sherman, Paris and Greenville are gone.

A major source of this commentary is Baseball-Reference.com. (MAP: WL)

Division 8

West of 7A and Northwest of Chapel

J.M. Lindsay: Converted Gainesville from a Community to a City (THM)

J.M. (James Menees) Lindsay (December 31, 1835–May 3, 1919) was so instrumental in the economic, religious and educational development of Gainesville that maybe it would have been more appropriate to rename Gainesville for Lindsay. Instead, the town four miles west of Gainesville bears his name.

Lindsay was born on December 31, 1835, in Wilson County, Tennessee, son of Reverend Lewis and June R. McFarland Lindsay. Lindsay's father was a missionary Baptist minister as well as teacher to his son.

Like a considerable number of southern attorney emigrants, J.M. was a graduate of Cumberland (Tennessee) Law School. Shortly after law school graduation, he left Tennessee with nineteen dollars in his pocket and headed for Texas. He traded his slow mule for a faster pony in Arkansas, arriving in Gainesville on his twenty-second birthday.

He opened a law office in a small frame house near the courthouse. In 1861, he was elected to the Texas legislature and was its youngest member. He was also a justice of the peace until he joined Company A of Fitzhugh's Regiment, Walker's Division of the Trans-Mississippi Department of the Confederate army. He was captured at the Battle of Pleasant Hill but was later exchanged for a Union soldier. He spent most of the Civil War in Arkansas and Louisiana.

After the war, he was a delegate to the Texas Constitutional Convention of 1866, which nullified secession and abolished slavery. He represented Cooke, Montague, Wise, Jack, Young, Clay, Wichita, Archer, Wilbarger, Baylor, Throckmorton, Hardeman, Knox and Haskell Counties at that convention. On November 3, 1868, Lindsay married **Tennie Bonner** (buried in Division 4). Her father was John Bonner, who had been a merchant in Tennessee prior to coming to Texas, first to Lamar County and later to Cooke County.

Lindsay was a member of the first city council of Gainesville when the city was incorporated in 1873. In 1874, Governor Richard Coke appointed him judge for the Sixteenth Judicial District, which covered Cooke, Grayson, Wise, Montague and other counties to the west. Later in the year, Judge Lindsay organized the first district court for Clay County. He only served one term as district judge, but "Judge Lindsay," as he was continually addressed afterward, made his primary mark as a financier, civic promoter and philanthropist.

As president of the Cooke County Agricultural and Mechanical Association, he was instrumental in organizing the first Cooke County Fair in 1871. He provided land on the south side of Gainesville for a subsequent county fair at Kanetso Park in 1897 and 1898.

Lindsay's habit of donating land for churches began in 1862 when James Peery, a recently converted Christian, asked him to donate land for the Cumberland Presbyterian Church. This two-room frame structure on the southwest corner of Denton and Church Streets later became the First Presbyterian Church.

On July 14, 1877, Judge Lindsay donated another piece of land out of his Lindsay Addition so the First Baptist Church could have the first building of its own. This land was later traded for a corner lot on Denton and Broadway Streets. Lindsay was ordained a deacon in this church on August 16, 1890. In 1884, he donated another lot for the construction of St. Paul's Episcopal Church on the northwest corner of California and Jefferson Streets.

Lindsay's first efforts at community building outside of Gainesville occurred in 1878 when he donated six acres of land for a school on the prairie twelve miles southwest of Gainesville. This piece of land became the nucleus of the community of Era.

He was a major influence in convincing Frederick Stevens to extend the Denison and Pacific Railroad from Denison to Gainesville in 1879, guaranteeing the future growth of Gainesville to the detriment of the future of Dexter. He donated right of way for the railroad from the old brickyard site to California Street.

In 1880, Lindsay organized the Gainesville Gas and Coal Company, capitalized at $50,000. He served as its vice-president. That was also the year the city began its operation of a public school system. Lindsay donated land on the south side of his home on Lindsay Street and financed the construction of the South School on that site (later to be J.M. Lindsay Elementary School).

In 1882, Lindsay and his associates founded Gainesville National Bank with a capital of $100,000. He was bank president until 1902, when the bank became Lindsay National Bank. The year 1882 also marked the completion of the construction of the Lindsay House, Gainesville's finest hotel for many years. It was the scene of many cattle deals in the heyday of the cattle business, and it hosted the Southwestern Cattle Raisers Association conventions of 1882 and 1888. Well-known cowmen like Shanghai Pierce and Charles Goodnight stayed there, as well as Joseph G. McCoy, who was instrumental in making Abilene, Kansas, the terminus for the Chisholm Trail.

Lindsay's further involvement in railroad expansion to the west resulted in the founding of the city of Lindsay. He was an original stockholder in the Gainesville, Henrietta and Western Railway, which was chartered on July 23, 1886, with the purpose of connecting Gainesville to Seymour, where the Western Trail crosses the California Trail.

The forerunner of Lindsay, Texas, was Lindsay Switch (1886), cattle-loading pens adjacent to the railroad five miles west of Gainesville. In January 1891, Judge Lindsay sold 3,500 acres of land in that area to Anton and August Flusche to develop a German community. Judge Lindsay retained 4,000 acres north of that site. On June 3, 1901, he gave 10 acres of land to the City of Lindsay for a park "for holding picnics and other public purposes." He also gave $300 toward the total cost of $800 for the construction of the first Catholic church built on the property that he had donated.

In 1892, Judge Lindsay bought Gainesville's mule-powered streetcar company to satisfy a judgment of $855 against it held by the Merchants National Bank of Fort Worth. The streetcar line had three miles of track that extended from the old North School (later site of Ben Franklin Elementary

School) in the northwest part of town, through the downtown area down California Street, east to Ritchey Street and eventually south to Kanetso Park on the south end of Lindsay Street.

Judge Lindsay was obviously one of the largest landowners in Cooke County. According to the Cooke County General Index to Deeds, from 1882 to 1885, he was the exclusive seller in ninety-seven real estate transactions and was a partner with others in forty additional real estate sales. Those other realtor partners were a Gainesville elite that included **William Hudson** (Division 19), **George Y. Bird** (Division 4), **W.O. Davis** (Division 12) and **F.M. Dougherty** (Division 12).

During his active years in business, Lindsay acquired over twenty thousand acres of land in Cooke, Grayson, Denton, Wise, Montague, Clay, Wichita and Hardeman Counties. He was the guiding light of the Gainesville Retailers Association, and he was also involved in the "Good Roads" movement.

At the time of his death at the age of eighty-three, his real estate holdings in Gainesville included the Lindsay House, *Gainesville Register* office, the Zacharias Building, the Tanner-Belden Store, the Chinese Laundry, the Majestic Theatre, the Gas Company Building and the building occupied by H. Bertram and Gulf Gasoline. He also owned some acreage in Chaves County, New Mexico, and an interest in oil and gas leases in Carter County, Oklahoma.

Judge Lindsay died on May 3, 1919. He was survived by his wife, **Tennie Bonner Lindsay** (Division 4); son, **Lewis B. Lindsay** (August 31, 1871–May 13, 1934); daughter, **Jimmie Tennie Embrey** (December 4, 1877–January 2, 1933); and two sisters, Mrs. Elizabeth Davis and Mrs. Ella L. Pendleton, both of Lebanon, Tennessee.

This narrative was used to justify an Official Texas Historical Marker for J.M. Lindsay's grave. (MAP: JL)

Division 8

East of 7, South of S and West of X

Killed Over Berry-Picking Privileges

Clifford A. Bosley (June 20, 1887–June 15, 1923), veteran of World War I, was shot to death in his blackberry patch by his cousin, B.C. Barney, because of Bosley's refusal to give Barney berry-picking privileges.

Barney's first trial before district judge C.R. Pearman in Gainesville resulted in a hung jury after thirty-seven hours of deliberation. One of the points in dispute at the trial was whether Bosley was pointing his shotgun at Barney when Barney shot Bosley. Bosley's sister, Martha Morgan, claimed her brother was unarmed although his shotgun lay nearby. Barney claimed that Bosley, in pointing his shotgun at him, announced, "I'm going to fill you so full of shot it will take a week to pick them out!" When Barney did shoot Bosley, Barney was not aware he had mortally wounded him. Shortly after the shooting, Barney walked to town to surrender to authorities because he thought "I did something wrong."

In an earlier dispute over Barney's right to reside on Bosley's property, Barney had won in justice of the peace court. According to Mrs. Barney, Bosley in a previous encounter with her had declared he "would like to beat her up so she couldn't get about for six months." Mr. Barney had talked to County Attorney Fred Wankan about formal legal action against Bosley, but Wankan had delayed about doing anything.

Part of the defense's testimony included remarks told to Barney prior to the shooting incident that Bosley had been in "the crazy house" and that he was mentally deficient because of being shell-shocked in World War I. (MAP: CB)

She Went to Jail for Keeping a Secret

On November 26, 1924, **Agnes Darrah Weaver** (b. 1881) finally escaped the controversy surrounding her and came home from Fort Worth to rest beside her infant son, **Richard K. Darrah** (d. September 12, 1919). Her anguish over the death of her child, whom friends said she never got over, probably contributed to her desire to protect the baby of Zelma Adams.

The case of Zelma Adams's baby made front-page headlines in 1923 in Dallas and Fort Worth. Zelma Adams, a former chorus girl, sought custody of the baby she had given up several years before after giving birth at a Fort Worth maternity home. Zelma took Agnes Darrah (later Mrs. Weaver) to court in Fort Worth to force her to reveal the location of Zelma's baby.

Agnes refused to reveal the name and whereabouts of the baby's foster mother in court. Agnes at the time was a proprietor of a rooming house on Main Street in Fort Worth. As a seriously ill invalid, she had to be carried into court on a stretcher to give her dramatic testimony. She went to jail for several days for contempt of court for refusing to divulge the location of the foster mother (who was in Los Angeles). She went on a hunger strike in jail and was finally released after telling state district Judge Lattimore of the whereabouts of the baby.

At the time of the trial, Agnes had custody of a young foster daughter, Baby Ruth, who some claimed may have been Zelma's baby. When authorities threatened to take Baby Ruth away from Agnes, Agnes admitted that the baby was her biological baby. The father, Will R. Weaver, a former Gainesville café owner, admitted he was the baby's father and married Agnes.

Will Weaver did not attend Agnes's funeral, according to the *Register*, because he was "too broken up." Baby Ruth and Agnes's sixteen-year-old son, Raymond Darrah, did attend. Also in attendance was the "mystery woman," the foster mother of Zelma's baby, who revealed she was a longtime friend of Agnes. She declared that if she had been forced to give up the Adams baby, "two hearts would have been broken instead of one."

Agnes had two funeral services. Father Murtaugh presided over her Fort Worth service, where he described her "last days as a real Christian." Baby Ruth played at the foot of the casket. Father Brady of St. Mary's Catholic Church presided over her graveside ceremony in Gainesville. (MAP: AW)

Mother of "My Blue Heaven's" Gene Austin

Serena Belle Austin (August 2, 1881–August 4, 1956) died at the home of her brother, George Harrell, in Madill, Oklahoma, after an illness of a couple of months. She had been a resident of California for many years.

Belle's previous married name was Lucas. She gave birth to Eugene Lucas on June 24, 1900, in Gainesville. He later took his stepfather's name and called himself "Gene Austin." Belle's famous son was a veteran of the military campaign against Pancho Villa in Mexico and a veteran of World War I. After pursuing a couple of other professions, Gene surrendered to the lure of a career as a songwriter and crooner.

He was very popular as a singer in the decades of the 1920s and 1930s. His Grammy award–winning song, "My Blue Heaven," sold over twelve million records in 1927. He returned to his hometown of Gainesville in 1940, where he was featured in a tent show for the Circus Roundup of the Gainesville Community Circus. A longtime resident of Las Vegas, he ran unsuccessfully for the governorship of Nevada in 1962.

The source of much of this information about one of Gainesville's famous sons is the *Handbook of Texas Online*. (MAP: BA)

Six-Year-Old Boy Died from Peanut Shell in His Lung

Tommy (Herman T.) Brooks (1924–March 30, 1930), son of **Harry J. Brooks Sr.** (1887–February 1944) and **Esther Bentley Brooks** (1892–October 1964), died from a lung infection after surgery to remove a peanut shell he had ingested into his lung while eating peanuts. According to an article in the *Gainesville Register*, two days after his parents thought he had coughed up the peanut shell, Tommy's wheezing resulted in his admission to the Gainesville sanitarium.

The *Register* described in detail the difficult operation to remove the peanut hull, performed by **Dr. E.C. Mead** (Division 15) and witnessed by his medical colleagues. X-ray was not precise enough to pinpoint the exact location of the obstruction. Using a bronchoscope, which "consists of a small tube, a light reflector and a pair of forceps which are inserted through the tube and operated mechanically by the surgeon," Dr. Mead probed one lung and then the other in the elusive attempt to remove the hull.

The procedure, which normally takes ten minutes, required one and a half hours. The operation had to be stopped once because Tommy stopped breathing and had to be resuscitated. Tommy was shown the bronchoscope and the peanut hull after his ordeal.

Sadly, Tommy died of a lung infection four days after his surgery. Children of First Presbyterian Church's Sunday School Department served as honorary pallbearers. (MAP: TB)

SUSPECTED MAD DOG INDIRECTLY RESPONSIBLE FOR THIS DEATH

James C. Jirasek (September 19, 1891–February 1, 1931), a prominent farmer who lived northwest of Gainesville, was accidentally shot on August 20, 1930. A stray dog that appeared rabid showed up on the homeplace, and when Madeleine (Mrs.) Jirasek went into the house to get a .22 rifle, the rifle discharged when it was dropped while her young son attempted to hand her the rifle. The bullet struck her husband, who was standing outside the house.

The bullet penetrated a vertebra between his shoulders and resulted in paralysis from the chest down. Surgeons at the hospital in Temple determined that the location of the bullet made his condition inoperable. He died in the Gainesville sanitarium a little more than five months after the accidental shooting.

Madeleine M. Jirasek (July 10, 1893–July 30, 1970) attended to her paralyzed husband almost continuously from the accident until his death, except for a brief period when she gave birth to J.C. Jirasek Jr. about three weeks before her husband's death. (MAP: JJ)

BOOTLEGGER PARDONED BY "MA" FERGUSON

William C. "Will" Price (November 11, 1872–December 8, 1946) is described in his obituary as a former barber and taxi driver in Gainesville. What his obituary does not say is that in 1924, Sheriff M.E. Elliott, led by the smell of prune mash, raided his home and smokehouse on North

Weaver Street. The law enforcement officers seized one quart of red whiskey, one half gallon of prune whiskey, the worm of a still and forty gallons of prune mash.

Will Price was successfully prosecuted by County Attorney Fred Wankan, who also was the head of the Cooke County Ku Klux Klan and a local Boy Scout leader. Will was subsequently sentenced to two years in the penitentiary for violating prohibition law; however, he never went to the penitentiary.

Governor "Ma" Miriam Amanda Ferguson was opposed to Prohibition and very generous with her pardoning power. She granted Will Price several furloughs to prevent him from going to the penitentiary. And upon recommendation of the district judge and county judge of Cooke County, she granted him a full pardon because of an illness. Price must have not been extremely ill, since he lived for another twenty years after his pardon.

According to the *Gainesville Register*, Ma Ferguson thought it appropriate to pardon a group of men prior to Thanksgiving Day. By November 25, 1926, Ma had granted five hundred full pardons. (MAP: WP)

His Third Resting Place

Joseph P. Davis Jr. (May 6, 1924–May 17, 1945) is one of numerous casualties of World War II whose families had difficulty finding the remains of their loved one to be finally interred in Fairview. Joseph's mother, **Gladys Ward Davis** (July 14, 1901–July 7, 1979), was notified over three and a half years after her son's disappearance on an aerial mission that he was buried in United States Armed Forces Cemetery Number 1 in Yokahama, Japan.

Flight Officer Davis was a solo pilot of a P-51 Mustang fighter whose final mission took him from Iwo Jima to be part of a sweep over Tasugi air base, twenty miles from Tokyo. He was last seen after completing his mission, eight miles south of his target. His plane crashed and burrowed in deep water in a rice paddy in the Kanagawa Prefecture, Island of Honshu.

Much later, a recovery team recovered his body and determined his identification from contents of a pocket. Serial numbers on the plane's machine guns identified the plane as his. Davis was temporarily buried in the United States Armed Forces Mausoleum Number 2 on Honshu. Later, he was reinterred in Yokahoma and finally buried a third time in Fairview. (MAP: JD)

Division 9

Famous Texas Aggie Athlete and Olympian

Jack F. Mahan (July 22, 1898–September 2, 1955) was a gifted Gainesville high school athlete who became regionally famous on the college gridiron at Texas A&M and received national recognition as a javelin thrower.

His high school senior yearbook, the *1916 Budget*, described Mahan's football prowess by proclaiming him to be the best fullback in Texas, despite "a lame ankle and boils." He endured much of the season and still "hit the line with the strength of Hercules. Many times he would carry the ball forward ten yards. His forward passes were accurate and true."

World War I interrupted his athletic accomplishments. The young Great War veteran played on coach D.X. Bible's legendary football team at Aggieland; they were undefeated, untied and unscored upon in 1919. In 1920, he was captain of the team, which only lost one game. He received All Southwest Conference honors at fullback both seasons.

Mahan was also a standout on the A&M track team. He represented the United States in the javelin throw in the 1920 Olympics in Antwerp, Belgium. Twenty-nine nations competed in the first Olympics after World War I. (The aggressor nations were not invited to participate.) This was the Olympics with two "firsts": the five-ring Olympic flag was flown over the games for the first time, and pigeons were released for the first time to symbolize peace. The Olympic facilities were not completed in war-torn Belgium when the athletes arrived, and the athletes slept on portable cots.

Mahan finished twelfth in the javelin throw. The top ten were finalists in the event, and the three medal winners were all from Finland. Coincidentally, Charles Paddock, who was born in Gainesville, was a track star of that Olympic games. The "fastest human" won first in the one hundred meters, second in the two hundred meters and anchored the gold-winning four-hundred-meter relay team.

After finishing at A&M, Mahan returned to Gainesville and operated a large farm for **J.D. Leeper** (Division 19) until he started his career as a vocational agriculture teacher at Gainesville High School. Jack continued his interest in football as part of a football officiating crew for the Southwest Conference, of which Texas A&M was a member.

In poor health for several years prior to his death, Mahan drowned in a stock tank on the Melvin Farr farm southeast of Gainesville. He apparently caught a fishing lure in his shoelaces, lost his balance and fell off an embankment into the water. His wife discovered his body when he failed to return home. (MAP: JM)

In the Line of Duty

In the Line of Duty is the title of an autobiography written by **Lewis Calvin Rigler** (August 7, 1914–June 25, 2009) and his daughter-in-law, Judyth Wagner Rigler, in 1984, describing his career of thirty-six years with the Texas Department of Public Safety, thirty years of that as a Texas Ranger. Rigler was born in Waco and spent his years growing up on a farm outside of Lorena. In 1933, he joined the Civilian Conservation Corps and helped build the Indian Lodge at Fort Davis and Bottomless Lake State Park in Roswell, New Mexico. Twenty-five dollars of his thirty-dollar-a-month wages was sent home to help his family. When he joined the army in 1935, he started his military service at the same place where he started his CCC service, at Camp Bullis in San Antonio.

He made Gainesville his home throughout his career as a Texas Ranger from 1947 to 1977. One of the most troubling cases he dealt with as a Ranger was the still unsolved mystery of Virginia Carpenter, who disappeared on her train trip from Texarkana to then Texas College for Women in Denton in the summer of 1948. Rigler also was assigned security detail at Market Hall for President Kennedy on the fateful day of November 22, 1963.

Cooke County Sheriff Mike Compton pays his respects at the grave of good friend, Texas Ranger Lewis Rigler, author of *In the Line of Duty*. *With permission of Sheriff Compton and Joyce Rigler.*

Although not physically intimidating, Ranger Rigler commonly transported criminals without resorting to handcuffs. He typically asked, "Do you want to be transported as a criminal or as a man?" No one violated Rigler's trust.

He was a best friend of Ranger Captain **Tom Hickman** (Division 4) and was with him when he died of cancer. (MAP: LR)

Division 10

Killed Falling from a Circus Train

James Nelson's monument is a medium-sized gray column with a bell-shaped top, located on the south side of Division 10 near the street. The marker inscription states: "**James Nelson**, died Oct. 23, 1910. Of Sells-Floto Show Company; Accidentally Killed falling from train (Sells-Floto Train); Remembered by his friends with the Sells-Floto Show Company." The Sells-Floto Show Company was a major circus in an era when many circuses traveled by rail. Nelson was manager of this circus.

Gainesville welcomed many circuses prior to having its own. Buffalo Bill came to Gainesville twice as part of a Wild West show and/or circus, once with Sells-Floto Show Company. Tom Mix also toured with the Sells-Floto Show Company in 1929. A former aerialist for Sells-Floto later trained some female trapeze artists for the Gainesville Community Circus. (MAP: JN)

Division 11

Suicide by Morphine

Richard M. Pulliam (d. January 9, 1893), employee of Gooding's Drug Store, died of a morphine overdose. Doctors Post and Black were unable to save him when contacted about two hours after he took the overdose in his room in back of the drugstore. The day before, the young clerk had received a letter that caused him some anguish, and he tore it up. The *Weekly Hesperian* conjectured, "Whether the rash deed was caused by disappointed love, financial trouble, drink, or insanity, we are unable to say." Pulliam's father, C.A.M. Pulliam of Memphis, Tennessee, sent word to bury him here "nicely" and send him the bill.

Suicide deaths by morphine were not uncommon in Gainesville hotels in the late 1800s and early 1900s. They were usually transients whose bodies were shipped home from Gainesville. Newspapers of that period commonly advertised a cure for morphine, opium, whiskey and heroin addiction. That was also the period of the "patent medicine cures." (MAP: RP)

Killed in Philippine Insurrection

Leonard Clyde Smith (July 1882–May 8, 1904) was the son of Mr. and Mrs. **Lenard** [*sic*] **B. Smith** (buried January 2, 1892, and September 16, 1886, respectively). Clyde apparently lied about his age to enlist in the United

This Kennedy family monument in Division 11 is a manufactured zinc monument. It was probably manufactured by the Monumental Bronze Company of Bridgeport, Connecticut. The company preferred the term "white bronze."

States Army in Oklahoma City on January 28, 1903, because he was not yet twenty-one, the minimum age to enter the army. His previous occupation was listed as railroad brakeman.

Private Smith of the Seventeenth Infantry was among seventeen of a fighting group of forty soldiers killed in ambush by Moro insurgents, Moslem rebels, at Simpetan on the Island of Mindanao in the southern Philippines. This was part of a continuing war the United States waged to try to bring order to the Philippines, which the United States acquired as a result of the Spanish-American War. The casualties in this jungle war were much greater than in the "Splendid Little War," a nickname for the Spanish-American War.

Clyde Smith's brother, R.R. Smith of Itasca, Texas, was notified by mail of his brother's death. His personal effects included five photographs, a writing tablet and package of envelopes and seventy-eight cents in Philippine postage stamps. In the military record is a description of Private Smith: 5 feet 7.5 inches, brown hair, brown eyes, two scars on his forehead and one scar on his cheek. Those scars were from a boyhood accident in which a glass cracker box fell off a shelf in Modrall's grocery store in Gainesville and cut his head severely.

Smith's body came by Santa Fe train from San Francisco. He was reburied in Fairview on April 1, 1905. Until recently, this grave was unmarked. Tom Carson, former owner of KGAF radio station and active participant in Gainesville's Host City annual program honoring Congressional Medal of Honor recipients, noticed this oversight and persisted in obtaining a proper grave marker from the Veterans Administration. His research is the basis for most of this article. That monument was dedicated on June 14, 2008, Flag Day. (MAP: CS)

Casualty of World War I, Killed in Ardmore

Edward B. Sullivan (d. July 7, 1918), who grew up in Gainesville, was killed in a training flight while taking off from Electric Park in Ardmore, Oklahoma, on his way back to Gainesville. Mechanic Ed C. Doyle of Grand Rapids, Michigan, riding with Sullivan, was also killed in the crash. Sullivan's airplane was one of three planes that had flown together from Barron Field in Fort Worth to Gainesville earlier in the day.

Sullivan had flown numerous times to Gainesville and enjoyed visiting friends while here. On this fateful day, mechanic G.B. Haskell, who flew with Sullivan from Fort Worth to Gainesville, decided not to go to Ardmore but to stay in Gainesville and visit friends. Mechanic Doyle took his place. Sullivan attempted to take off from Ardmore against a stiff wind. From about one hundred feet, the plane nose-dived to earth, bursting into flames upon impact. The two aviators burned while strapped in their seats.

The *Gainesville Register* eulogized Edward Sullivan in this way: "He did some of the most daring flying ever seen here…He was utterly fearless and his only wish no doubt would have been that he might have gone to his death fighting the Huns."

Sullivan's body lay in state at the home of **Otto Vaeth** (Division 20). Edward Sullivan's mother came from San Antonio. Gainesville mayor

J. Z. Keel (Division 15) issued a proclamation asking businesses and banks to close from 9:00 to 10:30 a.m. for the funeral. An overflow crowd witnessed the funeral at St. Mary's Catholic Church, and a long procession with military comrades as pallbearers took his body to rest near his father, **James Sullivan**, in Fairview.

Again, Tom Carson was responsible for obtaining a Veterans Administration grave marker for this previously unmarked grave. Additional inscriptions for both the Clyde Smith and Sullivan markers were donated by Richards Monument Company of Gainesville. (MAP: ES)

Died in Confederate Uniform Almost Sixty Years after the War Was Over

J.Y. Light (January 1, 1845–September 30, 1924), born in Waverly, Tennessee, left Fannin County, Texas, to join the Confederate army when he came of age. He and his wife, **Loucinda** (1845–November 3, 1886), lived

In Division 11, this ornate cast-iron grave cover marks the grave of infant Chevalier, buried August 1, 1910.

on a farm north of Gainesville beginning in 1885. J.Y. lived most of the last twenty years of his life with his son, Ira, at Electra, Texas.

At the time of his death, he was attending a state Confederate reunion in Fort Worth. He apparently got confused in a downtown crowd, wearing his replica Confederate uniform, and was fatally struck by a streetcar. His only wound was at the base of his skull. He was buried in his uniform. The *Register* described him as a "magnificent specimen of manhood, standing well over six feet and weighing more than 200 pounds. Light's hair and beard were cut in the style affected by General Nathan Bedford Forrest."

Light's funeral was originally scheduled in the morning at Gainesville's Santa Fe Depot, but the later arrival of his sister, Mrs. Charles Lee, from Peculiar, Missouri, forced the service to be held at graveside in the afternoon. The Masonic ritual was performed by Gainesville's Masonic lodge.

Tom Carson is responsible for bringing this story to light. (MAP: JL)

Division 12

W.O. Davis: Pioneer Attorney and Civic Leader THM

W.O. (William Owen) Davis (February 26, 1847–December 5, 1941) was born in Franklin, Heard County, Georgia. He was the fifth child of Lewis Franklin Davis and Elizabeth Ann Pittman Davis, natives of Georgia.

Davis's sense of public service was apparent at an early age. Despite being underage for military service, this seventy-pound, fourteen-year-old boy was successful in pestering a Confederate recruiting officer in allowing him to join the Confederate army. He served in Georgia's Company K, Fifth Infantry, Cummings's Brigade, Stephenson's Division, under General Hood and, later, in General Lee's Corps in the Army of Tennessee. One of his main duties was packing ammunition. After his company's surrender to General William T. Sherman in North Carolina in 1865, he returned home.

Shortly after being admitted to the bar in Georgia in 1870, Davis decided to come to Texas. His earliest impression of Texas, albeit a deceptive one, he received as a boy from a music teacher who paraded up and down the classroom aisles, beating time with his arms and singing, "It is springtime in Texas the whole year through."

Davis left Georgia thinking that Dallas would be his destination, but his trip took a circuitous route, winding up in Gainesville. The first leg of his trip he drove a six-horse freight wagon to Waxahachie. When he reached Dallas, he decided Dallas had enough attorneys. He went from there to McKinney and decided to investigate Decatur as a place to practice law. While he was in Wise County, a Kiowa and Comanche raiding party there discouraged him from staying. After a brief stay in Denton, he decided to try his luck in Gainesville. He walked most of the way until Dr. C.C. Usry, who lived about ten miles south of Gainesville, loaned him a horse to finish his trip. He arrived at this Red River valley community of about three hundred people on July 4, 1870.

Gainesville, as a fledgling settlement and jumping-off place for Indian Territory, had room for a young, enterprising attorney. Davis drafted the act of incorporation, making Gainesville an incorporated city in 1872. He was also a member of Gainesville's first school board.

During 1873–74, W.O. Davis served as one of four defense attorneys, representing **Theodore Schauseil** (Division 15), who was accused of killing a Marysville neighbor. After his first trial resulted in a hung jury, Schauseil was retried and sentenced to five years in the penitentiary. A petition for a pardon was immediately circulated and signed by many Gainesville and Cooke County citizens. Davis took the stage to Austin to deliver the request for a pardon to Governor Richard Coke. He promptly obtained his client's pardon.

Davis was first elected to the Texas Senate in a special election in March 1882 in order to replace the recently deceased Senator J.M. Martin of Cooke County. Senator Davis was sworn into office on April 6, 1882, the first day of a special session of the Seventeenth Legislature, which was called by Governor O.M. Roberts primarily to deal with the crisis caused by the capitol building's complete destruction by fire. Democrat Davis was reelected to a full four-year term in November 1882, easily defeating J.H. Reilley of the Greenback Party.

As chairman of the Senate Education Committee in the regular session of 1883, Davis was unsuccessful in his attempt to pass legislation to set aside the remainder of Texas's public land for the purpose of funding public education, but half of the remaining public domain was set aside for that purpose in the massive education reform law that passed in the special session of 1884. In addition, 1884 legislation earmarked twenty-five cents of the one-dollar poll tax on all male inhabitants between the ages of twenty-one and sixty to be used for public education.

Two interesting pieces of legislation passed during Davis's last regular session as a senator in 1885 deserve mentioning. One of those laws required all males between the ages of eighteen and forty-five—with the exceptions of invalids, ministers of the gospel, militiamen and volunteer firemen—to be responsible for the maintenance and repair of all public roads. The other law provided for an annual pension of $150 for any indigent veteran of the Texas War of Independence, any indigent signer of the Texas Declaration of Independence or indigent surviving spouse of either.

With the extension of the Missouri-Kansas-Texas (Katy) Railroad from Denison in 1879, Gainesville became a cattle boomtown. Davis's reputation as an astute attorney spread well beyond his Gainesville law office on the second floor of the office building on California Street (currently occupied by the *Gainesville Daily Register*). Numerous clients lived several days' travel from Gainesville by stage or horseback. They included ranchers from the Texas panhandle as far away as Amarillo and Canadian and those engaged in ranching operations under unique conditions in Indian Territory.

Davis argued at least three cases before the United States Supreme Court. The most interesting one was *Red River Cattle Company v. Sully* (1892). It originated in district court in Clarendon in 1885 and, after numerous appeals, finally reached the Supreme Court seven years later.

How did a case involving several North Texas ranchers' sale of 3,700 cattle to a New York City financier and railroad magnate wind up in the Supreme Court? It was a diversity of citizenship case involving parties from different states. Davis and H.E. Eldridge (Division 8) were the original attorneys for Red River Cattle Company, but Sawnie Robertson and Davis were the attorneys of record representing the cattle company before the Supreme Court. Robertson was experienced at practicing law before the high court. He was a former associate justice on the Texas Supreme Court and a personal friend of Jim Hogg. This was Davis's first Supreme Court case.

Red River Cattle Company was a corporation headquartered in Gainesville. The president of the corporation was Frank Houston of Terrell. Its two other principal stockholders were prominent residents of Gainesville. John H. Belcher, who lived in a large mansion on Belcher Street and donated land for the North School in Gainesville, was one of the area's most visible cattle kings. **Edwin T. Morris** (Division 3), the other major stockholder, was formerly sheriff of Cooke County from 1874 to 1878. Alfred Sully, the cattle buyer, maintained an office on Broadway in New York City. He was principal owner of the Long Island Railroad, president of the Ohio Southern Railroad and was in the process of becoming the largest individual stockholder in the Philadelphia and Reading Railroad.

The Red River Cattle Company sold Sully 3,700 head of cattle, which it owned on rangeland in Donley and Gray Counties. The deal was made on December 29, 1883, and Sully made complete payment at $22.50 a head in January 1884. It was his responsibility to round up the cattle in the spring of 1884. If he rounded up more than 3,700, he was supposed to pay for the additional cattle. If he rounded up fewer than 3,700, Red River Cattle Company was to make up the difference either in cash or cattle. At the conclusion of the roundup, Sully was short 779 cattle.

The dispute centered on a disagreement over whether the winter loss of cattle was Red River Cattle Company's loss or Sully's loss. Davis attempted to use Panhandle ranchers to verify an estimated loss of 25 percent of their herds in the unusually harsh winter of 1883–84, but the court in the first trial refused to use that evidence. Davis and the Red River Cattle Company ultimately lost their case before the Supreme Court on April 4, 1892. The court ruling in favor of Sully was largely based on the omission in the sale contract of a provision regarding the winter loss of cattle.

Nevertheless, Davis's successful law practice enabled him to build several brick buildings on California Street. He was also a bank director and acquired extensive landholdings, especially on the east side of Gainesville, extending to what is now known as Radio Hill.

His home was a brick Victorian mansion, built in 1891 at 505 South Denton Street. This Queen Anne–style residence featured gas lighting. Davis resisted converting to electric wiring, claiming that gas lighting was easier on the eyes and faulty wiring caused many house fires. This information runs counter to a popular myth that Davis, the outspoken political critic of **United States Senator Joseph Weldon Bailey** (Division 21), refused to have electric lights in his house because the local electric company displayed a portrait of Senator Bailey in its office.

Although not calling Bailey by name, in a 1906 *Gainesville Register* editorial entitled "The Boss," Davis referred to his subject as "addicted to poker, fast horses, good wine, and fast women." Davis played a leading role as one of Bailey's accusers in the 1907 special legislative committee's investigation of Bailey's behavior, although Bailey was officially exonerated.

In 1920, when Bailey was running for governor, Davis wrote a very caustic letter to the *Register* criticizing both Bailey and Mayor **J.Z. Keel** (Division 15). Davis intoned, "Keel has been Bailey's little dog here for years. Nothing makes Keel so happy as to be allowed to trot along in front of the senator barking and wagging his little tail and testing his new false teeth on everything that gets in the way." In response to the charge that Davis never speaks to Bailey, Davis claimed that when he and Bailey meet on the street, "He sees nothing below the tops of the telephone poles."

Approximately fifty years after his first service on the Gainesville city council in 1874, Davis was elected again to that body in the spring of 1925. In the fall of 1927, he made the motion to submit to the voters a plan for the creation of the city manager form of government and reducing the city council from ten to five members. That plan was approved by the voters, and in April 1928 he was elected as one of the five new aldermen. The council then selected Davis, who was eighty-one years old, to be mayor for that one-year term.

According to local attorney Shelby Fletcher, during the 1920s, W.O. Davis had a domino game interrupted by a telegram from Governor Dan Moody, offering him a place on the Texas Supreme Court. Davis rejected the offer because of his age.

Gainesville's "Grand Old Man" died on December 5, 1941. This distinguished jurist's life was just two days short of spanning the period from the Civil War to World War II. According to Gainesville attorney L.V. Henry, news of the attack on Pearl Harbor caused a stir during Davis's funeral at his home on South Denton Street. (MAP: DA)

Belle Favor Davis (October 24, 1850–July 11, 1885) was the first wife of W.O. Davis.

Much of this narrative was originally part of the application process for a Texas Historical Marker.

A Suffragette for Governor Hobby

Anna Underwood Davis (February 13, 1864–July 20, 1951), W.O. Davis's second wife, as president of the Cooke County Equal Suffrage Association, encouraged the voter registration of women in 1918 under a new Texas law that allowed women to vote in the Democratic primary (not the general election). She also organized a women's "Hobby for Governor" Club. Winning the Democratic primary in those days was tantamount to winning in the general election, because Republican candidates were rare.

According to her tombstone, "She Walks in Beauty." Who was responsible for this epitaph? Her husband preceded her in death a decade earlier. (MAP: DA)

WIFE OF ERA'S "FAVORITE SON," EWING THOMASON

Belle Davis Thomason (1883–May 1921), daughter of **W.O. and Belle Favor Davis,** married her father's law partner, Ewing Thomason, in 1905. He grew up in Era and returned to Cooke County in 1900 to practice law after graduating from the University of Texas Law School. He became a law partner of W.O. Davis and was county attorney from 1903 until 1907.

The clasped hands of Henry and Sallie Belcher in Division 12 symbolize a successful life together.

In 1911, he and his wife moved to El Paso to escape the threat of malaria. In 1919, in his second term in the Texas House of Representatives, he was elected House Speaker. Running for governor, he was eliminated in the first Democratic primary in 1920 by **Joseph Weldon Bailey** (Division 19) and Pat Neff. Belle died in El Paso in 1921. She and Ewing had two children.

Ewing became a fourteen-term member of the United States House of Representatives. In 1947, President Truman appointed Ewing to the federal bench. (Truman is the only president to visit Gainesville while in office, although he did not touch the ground. He spoke off the end of a caboose for a brief stop in front of the Santa Fe Depot in his "whistle-stop" campaign of 1948.) (MAP: BT)

Division 13

Ferryman Stabbed to Death on Halloween Night 1916

Tom Brown (d. October 31, 1916; buried November 6, 1916), the operator of Brown's ferry on Red River, seven miles north of Gainesville, was apparently stabbed to death during a drunken party on Halloween night near his cabin on Red River. County Attorney Owen Davis and Deputy Sheriff Charles Compton discovered Brown's body with a fatal stab wound above his knee two days after his death. Brown was approximately forty years old and was single. He was buried in Fairview when no one claimed his body.

The chief suspect in his death was Dick Blackburn, a companion of Tom Brown, who had two stab wounds in his shoulder. According to the *Register*, Blackburn, who had "partaken too freely of John Barleycorn," could not remember the details of the incident. (MAP: TB)

Division 14

"The Curtain Falls and the Last Act Is Done"

F.E. Collard (d. October 31, 1893) was a member of a touring drama company that had recently performed at the local opera house. The following is an excerpt from the *Weekly Hesperian*, November 3, 1893, to illustrate the tone and style of the time. (MAP: FC)

> *AN ACTOR'S DEATH*
> *The Curtain Falls and the Last Act Is Done*
>
> *F.E. Collard, a member of the Harper-Collard troupe, died at the LaClede hotel about midnight Tuesday night. He had been sick for several days and the troupe had been forced to leave him here.*
>
> *Mr. Collard, we learn, was a Christian gentleman who was respected by all who knew him. Mrs. Harper, his sister reached here yesterday morning. She was crazed with grief.*
>
> *The sad fate of the young man dying among strangers touched the hearts of many of our people and a goodly number of them followed the remains to their resting place in our cemetery.*
>
> *Revs. Harris and Pierce attended the funeral, and many of our best people went in the procession. The employees of the opera house acted as pall bearers, while the Texas State band marched in front of the hearse and discoursed sad, sweet music on the way to the cemetery.*

"Hospitality Chief"

David H. Turner (January 9, 1820–April 15, 1894) had a long career as a hotel manager and hotel owner in Gainesville. Turner, a native of Lynchburg, Virginia, came to Gainesville in 1880 via Pilot Point to manage the LaClede Hotel on the corner of Dixon Street and Broadway. A little over a year later, he quit the hotel business, buying a one-and-a-half-story residence on the corner of California and Jefferson Streets. Former guests of the LaClede Hotel, after socializing on Turner's front porch and usually enjoying dinner with him, convinced Turner to convert his home to a hotel in 1884. Turner added a kitchen and dining room to the east wing of his house, which he transformed into Turner Cottage. Eventually five more rooms were added, and his son **Edgar** (buried March 4, 1941) took over management in 1892. His son **Luther** (Division 19) joined his brother in the hotel business in 1902.

This information is from *First 100 Years in Cooke County* and the *Gainesville Daily Register*. (MAP: TU)

A "Sporting" Woman

Nora Wilson (d. May 31, 1910) is identified in the funeral records of George Carroll and Son as a "sporting" woman. A "sporting" woman was a nice way of saying she was a professional between the sheets. Being convicted of maintaining a "disorderly house" also did not mean she was a poor housekeeper. Nora died of suicide by taking carbolic acid in Ardmore, Oklahoma. While many persons from the north side of Red River came to marry here, some came to be buried here. (MAP: NW)

The Only Female State Pure Food Inspector in 1916

Elizabeth "Lizzie" Lee Darwin (1867–April 13, 1916), daughter of **Captain** and **Mary Ann Lee** (Division 19) and widow of **Percy Darwin** (1861–March 19, 1893), died suddenly after being stricken with spinal meningitis on a shopping trip to Dallas. She died at the home of her brother, John, in Dallas, surrounded by family.

Lizzie was the only female chief inspector for the State Pure Food Department and had worked in that capacity for several years. The *Temple Daily Telegram* referred to her recent visit there professionally and declared she was "a devoted teacher, club woman, civic worker and constant laborer in the Lord's vineyard for improving the conditions of humanity and the betterment of mankind generally." A resolution from the Civic League of Wichita Falls also made similar remarks about her.

She remained single after the death of her husband and had no children. (MAP: ED)

Legendary Cooke County Sheriff Killed by a Train

H.P. (Henry Patrick) "Pat" Ware (October 15, 1855–December 1, 1928), the longtime pioneer sheriff of Cooke County, was killed by a Katy passenger train as his Ford coupe stalled on the tracks. His automobile was pinned between the passenger train and some rail cars on a railroad siding in front of the passenger station. Pat Ware probably did not hear the approaching train. He had just visited the sickbed of one of his best friends, Sheriff **Jake Wright** (Division 21).

Pat Ware was a three-month-old baby when he came to the Woodbine area with his parents, John and Nancy Ware, via covered wagon from Springfield, Missouri. John Ware died fighting for the Confederacy and left a wife and six sons: Pat, Jim, Elijah, **Rad** (Division 22), Spence and John. On January 6, 1878, Pat married **Matilda E. Anderson** (September 27, 1857–January 28, 1934) at the Ware homeplace near Woodbine. They moved to Gainesville in 1884.

Pat Ware began his career in law enforcement, first as deputy sheriff and then as a Gainesville city constable. He was sheriff of Cooke County from 1887 to 1895 and 1903 to 1911. His immense reputation was not due strictly to his longevity as sheriff but also to his reputation at apprehending criminal offenders. He was a large, imposing figure as a law enforcement officer. Because of Gainesville's proximity to Indian Territory, a popular refuge for desperadoes, the sheriff spent much of his time traveling to capture fugitives and transferring fugitives to other law enforcement jurisdictions and the penitentiary.

On the left, seated, is Marcus Webster, first sheriff of Cooke County, 1849; on the right is Sheriff Pat Ware, nine-term sheriff in the late 1800s. *Courtesy of Morton Museum of Cooke County.*

Here is a sample of a detailed missing person report involving a Baptist minister from Leon, Indian Territory, published by Sheriff Ware in an 1894 issue of the *Dallas News*:

> *G.G. Doyal is 43 years old, 6 feet high, light complexion, blue eyes, left eye is defective, caused by being burnt by powder, weighs 180 pounds, and had with him the following described wagon and team: One red-sorrel mare mule, 5 years old, 15 hands high, flax mane and tail; one light bay mare mule, round body, small black spot on her hip; one new Studebaker wagon, California brake, feed box fastened to the hind gate, back part of spring seat broken.*

In January 1888, the *Hesperian* joked about an encounter Sheriff Ware had riding a bucking horse and came to the conclusion that it was easier to catch a pony thief than to ride a pony:

> *Our good natured Pat, who has a state wide reputation of being the best sheriff in Texas…while on his way up Commerce Street going to dinner, a friend kindly offered him the service of a pony to assist the genial sheriff in steering through the mud. Pat mounted the inoffensive looking animal, which in an instant seemed to recognize the fact that it was in the clutches of the law, where upon it made a break for liberty. It bucked, reared, tore, snorted, kicked and cavorted, until finally the sheriff and his captive parted, one going heavenward and the other going northward. Pat being of an angelic turn of mind moved upward towards the New Jerusalem, and approached so near that he could hear the rustling of wings, but when he lit, oh, mud and slush! You were knocked out of time on the first round. Friends came to the rescue and assisted in the resurrection of Cooke County sheriff who had enough mud sticking to his wardrobe to start a land boom in the Panhandle.*

Pat Ware was not a member of any church; however, he had one of the longest funeral processions in Gainesville's history. He had approximately one hundred honorary pallbearers. (MAP: PW)

Six of Their Children Died at an Early Age

Judge J.P. Hall (March 25, 1841–November 26, 1929) and his wife, **Hephziba "Hepsa" Elmira (Hancock) Hall** (February 8, 1844–November 13, 1925), were parents of six children who all died at a very young age, illustrating the difficulty of raising children past childhood in the late 1800s. The Hall children, in the chronological order of their deaths, were: **Susan Madora** (October 1, 1861—June 9, 1871), **John Clark** (August 15, 1872–September 18, 1876), **Jimmie** (June 23, 1874–February 9, 1877), **Fannie Bell** (November 30, 1869–July 26, 1877), **infant** (b. and d. October 14, 1879) and **Walter** (July 25, 1881–May 5, 1883).

Judge Hall was born near Enlaw in Green County, Alabama. Upon completion of his schooling there at the age of sixteen, he was hired to take charge of the school from which he had just graduated. He taught there for three semesters. He met his future wife while visiting sisters in Mississippi.

In March 1862, he joined Company H of the Thirty-first Mississippi Regiment in the Confederate infantry. He later achieved the rank of third lieutenant in cavalry under Captain Irby in Governor Robert Lowery's regiment.

Hall and his family, along with cousin Joshua Quarles, came to Upshur County, Texas, as part of a wagon train that traveled one thousand miles over thirty-four days. He and some cousins finally came to Cooke County from Smith County in East Texas. From 1871 until 1878, he and his family lived in Dexter and then moved to Gainesville.

Hall spent a little over three decades as a public servant, first as county judge from 1879 to 1887 and 1895 to 1899 and later as justice of the peace from 1917 to 1929.

On his eighty-fifth birthday, he was honored by Gainesville's First Baptist Church. He had been a member of that church since 1878, and he compiled a history of the First Baptist Church shortly before his eighty-fifth birthday. (MAP: JH)

WORLD WAR II TRAINING CASUALTY

Captain James Herman Kaden (October 27, 1917–May 7, 1943), commanding officer of the Fifteenth Reconnaissance Squadron of the U.S. Air Corps, was killed in a training flight near Bowling Green, Kentucky. According to a witness, his plane caught fire and he probably first thought of trying to land it. Captain Kaden parachuted too late at about three hundred feet. His chute partially opened, and he died of a broken neck. His nephew, Kenneth Kaden, recently described the plane as a trainer with a reputation of a "widow-maker."

At the time of the accident, Captain Kaden was stationed at Fort Knox, Kentucky. He entered the air corps in September 1941 and received his "silver wings" at Stockton Field, California, after graduating from Texas A&M with a bachelor's degree in landscape architecture. His military service took precedence over joining the Kaden family's horticulture business. Prior to being stationed in Kentucky, he had been stationed at Pine Camp near Carthage, New York.

An outstanding graduate of Gainesville High School, he was a two-time president of his high school's Hi-Y chapter. He also organized a Hi-Y chapter at Booker T. Washington High School and was elected state Hi-Y president. Son of **Otto** and **Dart Kaden**, he married Minnie Mae Voelkel, former Gainesville High School and junior college physical education teacher. He was also survived by a four-month-old son, Hayden James Kaden. (MAP: JK)

Killed in Vietnam Three Weeks Prior to End of Enlistment

One difference between the Vietnam War and previous wars was that the Defense Department was prompt in notifying next of kin concerning a death and prompt in sending the remains back home. Specialist-4 **Jerry Lynn Steed** (December 28, 1945–June 24, 1967) was killed by a Viet Cong mortar attack during a fierce battle on June 24, 1967, and his body arrived in Gainesville one week later for burial.

Specialist Steed was a graduate of Gainesville High School but lived with his mother, **Vera Nichols Steed** (September 19, 1909–January 14, 1973) in Wichita Falls at the time of his enlistment. He was stationed one year in Germany prior to his service in Battery C, Third Battalion of the Eighteenth Artillery, U.S. Army, in Vietnam. Jerry's death occurred three weeks before the end of his enlistment. Following the usual journalistic practice, Specialist Steed's death did not receive as much attention in the *Gainesville Register* as the death of actress Jayne Mansfield. Jerry's father, **Charley Lee Steed** (August 31, 1908–August 31, 1958), preceded him in death. (MAP: JS)

Division 15

Participant in the "Great Hanging"

James B. Davenport Jr. (August 22, 1839–March 11, 1920), sheriff at the time of the "Great Hanging" of 1862, helped select the hanging jury at the insistence of Colonel Young, an instrumental figure in this tragic episode. Davenport had just recently been elected sheriff in August preceding the "Great Hanging." He had moved to Cooke County in 1857 with his father, who had been a slaveholder in Missouri.

Davenport was later the captain of the Twenty-second Texas Cavalry and, much later, married the deceased Young's daughter, **Margaret** (August 26, 1859–December 29, 1907). Note a twenty-year difference in their ages. Most of this information is from Richard McCaslin's *Tainted Breeze*. (MAP: JD)

Another Participant in the "Great Hanging"

J. Pope Long (February 10, 1815–September 28, 1889) was also a jury member in the "Great Hanging." According to McCaslin's *Tainted Breeze*, Long was born in Kentucky and moved with his parents to Missouri. He was a surgeon in John C. Fremont's regiment during the Mexican War; however, he preferred the occupation of farmer as a civilian. He moved his family with five slaves to Sivells Bend in northwest Cooke County in 1861. Other family members are buried with him. (MAP: PL)

GAINESVILLE, HOME OF MANY OUTSTANDING DOCTORS, SOME IN THE SAME FAMILY

Jacob Edward Gilcreest, MD (August 29, 1850–March 18, 1926), was a pioneer physician and surgeon in Cooke County who was known professionally statewide. (He and his family names are misspelled with one "e" on their tombstones.) J.E. was born in Centersville, Georgia, and attended Louisville Medical College briefly but quit due to financial hardship and came to Gainesville. A Cooke County medical examining board "issued him the first certificate to practice medicine in Cooke County" even though he hadn't finished medical school. He did graduate from Louisville Medical College in 1879 and returned to Gainesville with his medical degree and new wife, the former Emma Catherine Looney of Louisville, Kentucky.

According to the *Gainesville Daily Hesperian* in 1888, his office was located in the drugstore that he also operated on the north side of the courthouse square. Not only could you have the services of a physician and surgeon, but he also offered a "great profusion of perfumes, soaps and toilet goods."

Dr. J.E. Gilcreest was one of the organizers of the Cooke County Medical Society in 1890. In December 1894, he was one of the hosts of a large two-day meeting of the North Texas Medical Association in Gainesville. After a long day's session of sharing medical knowledge, the doctors adjourned to Bartlett and Keeler's Oyster Parlor.

He was also active in the Texas State Medical Association and became its president in 1905. In 1909, Governor Thomas M. Campbell appointed him to the first state board of health. Dr. Jacob Edward Gilcreest also was the first president of the faculty of the University of Dallas Medical Department, the forerunner of Baylor College of Medicine in Dallas.

In his later years, he and his wife, **Emma Catherine** (February 13, 1849–December 24, 1937), lived with a daughter in Ennis. Emma Catherine's widowed mother, **Mary Ann Looney** (April 28, 1825–March 28, 1903), was a driving force in the creation of St. Mary's Catholic Church in Gainesville. Prior to that time, the Gilcreest home regularly hosted Catholic Mass.

Also buried here is their eldest son, **Edgar Lorrington Gilcreest, MD** (November 29, 1882–December 6, 1964), who also had a prestigious medical career. Edgar was a graduate of Johns Hopkins University Medical School. He served in the Serbian Red Cross in 1913 during the Turco-Balkan War.

Prior to the United States' entry into World War I, he worked for the American Red Cross in England, Italy and France. The *Gainesville Register* carried an interview Edgar had in New York after coming back from France in November 1915. Due to a large loss of a British elite in their prime, he suggested the United States should have a military draft so "the drones and doubters" shouldn't be left behind "to perpetuate a race." He also reported that in the winter a large percent of soldiers had been hospitalized for frostbite and frozen feet rather than battle wounds and that there were three classes of military hospitals: field hospitals "to save lives," clearance hospitals "to save limbs" and base hospitals "to make repairs."

During World War I, the Council of National Defense picked him and two others from the Southern Medical Association to advise that group in enlisting doctors to aid the war effort. He served for more than two years in base camp hospitals and evacuation hospitals. Edgar was awarded five battle stars for his participation in the Battles of the Second Marne, Somme, St. Mihiel, Argonne and Aisne. He was promoted from lieutenant to major.

After the war, he was on the faculty of the University of California Medical School. He died in Long Beach, California. Much of this information is in the *Handbook of Texas Online*. (MAP: GI)

Survivor of the Sinking of the *Lusitania*

Robert James Timmis Sr., who died at the age of seventy-four on August 8, 1939, was a hero as a passenger on the British liner the *Lusitania* when it was sunk by a German U-boat on May 7, 1915, shortly before the United States' entrance into World War I.

Timmis was a native of Liverpool, England. He came to the United States in 1887 and came to Gainesville in 1899. He was a cotton buyer who lived in a handsome residence at 116 East Church Street.

A Gainesville friend, Ralph Moody, who accompanied Timmis on that fateful voyage, drowned. The story is told that Timmis gave his life jacket to a lady, hit his head when jumping from the ship and swam for several hours before being picked up. He eventually became blind from his head injury. He still enjoyed swimming in the Gainesville pool, and he still crossed the Atlantic a total of seventy times and the Pacific eight times.

R.J. Timmis Sr. was an English cotton buyer and resident of Gainesville. He survived the sinking of the British passenger liner the *Lusitania*, which was sunk by a German U-boat prior to the United States' entrance into World War I. *Courtesy of Morton Museum of Cooke County.*

Robert James Timmis Jr. died tragically at the age of twenty-nine a little less than two months after his father's death on September 27, 1939. He died of an infection three days after emergency appendectomy surgery in Gainesville. He and his brother, Richard, were partners in Timmis Motors, an Oldsmobile car dealership. (MAP: TI)

One of the Youngest Licensed Pilots in the United States Died at Age Seventeen

Ralph Timmis (February 14, 1914–August 15, 1931) died after a seven-month struggle with pneumonia, pleurisy and other medical complications. His doctors, including Dr. Whiddon, brought an oxygen tent from Dallas to treat him. That failing, he was moved to the Scott and White Hospital in Temple, where he died. Members of the Newsome Dougherty High School, class of 1931, met at the Cooke County Library to attend Ralph's funeral as a group. The funeral was held at the Timmis home on Church Street.

Ralph and his twin, Richard, who were recent graduates of Newsome Dougherty High School, received student pilot certificates in February 1930,when they were sixteen years old. They were believed to be the youngest licensed pilots in the United States. Their flying instructors were the local Cassady brothers, Emmett and George. (MAP: TI)

Pioneer Builder

John Grundy Garrett (August 19, 1858–1919), originally a cabinetmaker, was a self-taught architect who became a prolific builder of fine Victorian homes, responsible for more than two hundred in a twenty-five-year period from the mid-1880s. He was in charge of the construction of First Methodist Church at 214 South Denton Street in Gainesville from 1892 to 1893 (a Texas Historic Landmark). Garrett was the architect for the **Frances Dougherty** and **Giles Houston** (Division 19) house at 604 South Denton Street in Gainesville in 1898. That Texas Historic Landmark, which has solid brick walls, also has twelve rooms and nine fireplaces. Garrett's architectural company, a partnership with a man named Collins, was the supervising architect for the beaux-arts Cooke County Courthouse, built in 1910, which is also a Texas Historic Landmark.

Garrett, son of **Robert H.** and **Wilmuth C. (Stark) Garrett** (Division 15), was born in Tippah County, Mississippi but moved to Tennessee with his family when he was eight years old. He learned cabinetmaking from his father. As a young adult, he and his parents moved to Texas, spending two years in Hill County prior to moving to Gainesville in 1884. He arrived here at the right time for the construction trade due to the wealth generated by the "cattle boom" days.

In 1887, he married **Ruth E. Hill** (Division 15), whose father, A.M. Hill, was a farmer and one-term sheriff from 1884 to 1886. Garrett was a Gainesville alderman from 1900 to 1906. He belonged to the well-known fraternal orders of his day: Woodmen of the World, Knights of the Maccabees and Knights of Pythias. (MAP: JG)

Another Cain and Abel Story

The death of **Sam McAdams** (April 21, 1848–September 2, 1889) is detailed under the headline "Passed Over the River" in the September 3, 1889 issue of the *Hesperian*. Sam was mortally wounded by his brother Jim in a dispute over the ownership of some cattle in Cottle County. He was shot in the back. The .44-caliber ball passed through his fourth lumbar vertebra. He lingered for over five weeks before dying in Gainesville in the home of Mrs. McCarty. Jim McAdams was out on a $1,500 bond for the assault prior to his brother's death. (MAP: SM)

Lawyer Killed in Fall from Office Window

Ed F. Finch (September 21, 1858–May 1, 1896), a local attorney originally from Missouri, was fatally injured from a fall out of his second-story office window. Suffering from a fainting spell and a chill, Finch called out from his second-story window to Dr. Ingle on the sidewalk below, asking for a "refreshing drink." The attorney fell out the window and rolled down an iron awning to the pavement below.

He was immediately carried to the rear of Bradley's lunch stand, where he was attended to by Doctors Block and Gilcreest. He died several days later from internal injuries. R.R. Bell, Judge Hayworth and George Dayton were in the office and witnessed the incident. This account is from several stories in the *Hesperian*. Ed shares a headstone with **G.G. Finch** (February 28, 1866–August 23, 1894). (MAP: EF)

German Emigrant and Indian Interpreter

Theodore Schauseil (March 12, 1838–October 3, 1920), a prolific storyteller, had much to talk about toward the end of his life. The *Gainesville Register* proclaimed on the occasion of his death, "There closed a chapter of human endeavor which compares with the most thrilling epochs of pioneer history." The following account of his life is taken from a two-part autobiographical story that appeared in the *Gainesville Register* on October 5 and 9, 1920, immediately after his death.

Theodore Schauseil was the son of nobleman, born in the province of Saxony in Germany. As a young man, he traveled to North Africa and Turkey to study archaeology and also studied briefly in Paris. He was punished by being confined in a German fortress for a time because of his participation in a duel.

Schauseil chose to escape his troubles by coming to America. He first settled in Davenport, Iowa, then Chicago and later still in rural Illinois until he decided to bring himself and his father to Texas. They finally located in Sadler's Bend in Cooke County. Theodore's father died there. Unable to obtain a coffin for his father, Theodore constructed one out of the "greasy boards of a kitchen table."

Schauseil's neighbors commonly referred to him as a "Dutch Yankee… where reconstruction had not wholly reconstructed [Cooke County] especially up about Schauseil's cabin on Fish Creek."

Schauseil tried to intercede for his employee, W.R. Cobb, who was supposedly competing with a neighbor, R.S. Richardson, for the romantic attention of a young lady. Cobb shot and killed Richardson and wounded his brother with Schauseil as a surprised witness. Cobb conveniently fled the area. A mob of approximately forty surrounded Schauseil's cabin with the intention of hanging him. Schauseil escaped the mob and surrendered to the authorities in Gainesville.

Theodore Schauseil's first trial in district court in Gainesville resulted in a hung jury. His second trial resulted in his receiving a five-year sentence. However, with much public support, his attorney, **W.O. Davis** (Division 12), acquired a pardon for him from the governor in November 1874.

Since Schauseil lost his home due to the legal cost of defending himself, he left Cooke County to go to work for General Ranald McKenzie at Fort Sill to serve as an interpreter in dealing with the Comanches, Kiowas and Apaches. The Indians nicknamed Schauseil "Muley Chief." He was a regular companion of Chief Kicking Bird. On one occasion, General McKenzie rescued Schauseil from a possible agonizing death by Comanches who turned against "Muley Chief" while he was escorting them west of Fort Supply, near Mount Sheridan. Schauseil's life was only half over at this point. (MAP: TS)

"THE FLORIST"

Herman Kaden (1861–January 11, 1938), an emigrant from Dresden, Germany, on November 26, 1883, founded a florist business that would eventually become the oldest continuously operating business under one family ownership in Gainesville, now involving the fifth generation of Kadens.

As a young man, Herman studied the science and art of the floral business in Lucerne, Switzerland, and Lyons, France. His journey from Germany to Gainesville was via New York City, with a temporary stay in St. Louis, where he answered an ad in the Gainesville *Hesperian* for a gardener for the John Stone ranch west of Gainesville. With that job, he saved enough money, $258, to buy approximately nine acres of land south of Gainesville.

Some of Kaden's original handiwork involving the botanical business still survives. The original greenhouse is still functional, and an underground cellar for the storage of flowers was functional for approximately one hundred years. Also, the original growing facility included hand-dug cisterns for the collection of rainwater.

"H. Kaden, the Florist" became a major supplier of cut flowers in the North Texas area, and in 1920, Kaden became a member of the Florist Telegraph Delivery Service, which originated in Michigan in 1910.

Herman's marriage to **Julia Schauseil** (1861–April 10, 1941), also born in Germany, produced male descendants who would ensure the continuation of the business beyond the lifetime of its founder. Julia grew up in the Marysville area and was the sister of **Theodore** and **Antoine Schauseil** (Division 15). Each of Julia and Herman's three sons—Theodore, Carl and **Otto** (Division 14-A)—specialized in a different aspect of the business. Grandson Wilson and great-grandson Kenneth, who continued the family tradition, received bachelor degrees in landscape architecture and floriculture, respectively, at Texas A&M.

Much of this information was provided by Kenneth Kaden and originally appeared in *Cooke County History: Past and Present*. (MAP: KA)

EDUCATOR, GRAIN DEALER, MAYOR

John Z. Keel (January 23, 1853–February 10, 1931) stayed behind in Missouri as a teenager when his family moved to Texas. He stayed to attend the prestigious Priychet Institute in Glasgow, Missouri, and marry **Mollie Patrick** (February 27, 1854–January 31, 1916) in 1876. Then he came to Gainesville, where he organized a private school that he and Professor A.B. McCans operated for a number of years in the Christian church on Belcher Street. That school featured the "first patented" school seats in this part of Texas.

He left the field of education to go into the grain business, and his son **Virgil** (Division 21) later joined him as a partner. Their grain business flourished. J.Z. was a charter member of the Texas Grain Dealers Association when it was organized in Fort Worth in 1898 and later served as its president.

He was a two-term alderman on the Gainesville City Council prior to serving as mayor from 1914 to 1920, during the tumultuous period of World War I. J.Z. was an ardent supporter of **Senator Joseph Weldon Bailey** (Division 21), and he hosted a huge rally in his grain elevator when Senator Bailey announced his candidacy for governor in 1920. (MAP: JK)

Division 16

Bawdy House Entrepreneur?

Grace "Gracie" Lane (buried March 10, 1910) lies in an unmarked grave close to Lovie Borne's marked grave in Division 16. According to the *Hesperian* of January 11, 1895, Gracie's fifteen-room house of ill repute in the "Silver City" area of Gainesville burned to the ground. She, however, was not the queen of the "soiled doves," the term for prostitutes of that era. That "honor" belonged to Ida Winter, who later in the year pled guilty to one of many charges and agreed to leave town and never return.

The *Hesperian* moralized, "It rids our county of the queen of the demimodes [demimondes] and will make it easier to deal with the others, for she was a hard fighter when taken to the courts." In January 1888, twenty-one "soiled doves" were fined $7.70 each for committing "vagrancy." (MAP: GL)

Katy Brakeman Killed in Derailment

John Charles Braswell (December 19, 1900–October 19, 1918) was killed when eight cars of eastbound Katy local #50 derailed one mile east of Woodbine. Charles was riding on top of one of the cars that derailed. He had just finished his apprenticeship as student brakeman and was on his way to Denison to go on the extra board as a brakeman. Charles was taken to Whitesboro, where he died one and a half hours after the accident and two months shy of his eighteenth birthday. His funeral was held at the home of his mother, **Mrs. Tommie Seagraves** (February 16, 1867–August 3, 1949), on the corner of Scott and Culberson Streets. His grave marker identifies him as "Our Baby." (MAP: JB)

Division 17

Unique Woodmen of the World Marker

W.H.M. Tuttle (May 13, 1864–December 29, 1897) has a unique Woodmen of the World grave marker. It features a large ball with the Woodmen insignia resting on feet at the top of a column. (MAP: WT)

German-American Craftsman, "A Good American"

This story of the life of **Augustus "Gus" Meyer** (January 31, 1851–September 1, 1948) is based on a *Register* article written by H.K. Lyde of Sherman, a deceased grandson of Meyer. Gus Meyer, native of Germany, left there in 1867 because of his opposition to compulsory military service. He landed in Philadelphia and, after learning English and making enough money as a teamster, decided to venture west. Meyer eventually made his way to Gainesville in a horse-drawn wagon.

Gus came to Gainesville from the north, and he fell in love at first sight when he stopped at the edge of town and a blue-eyed young blonde with a beautiful smile gave him a cool drink of well water under a big oak tree. In recounting this story to his grandson, Gus also described this young lady as having broad shoulders. His grandson commented to "Gramps" that he wasn't looking for a horse but a girl. Grandpa Meyer corrected him, "In those days the woman needed to be as strong as the man."

Young Gus told this girl, **Mary A. Knippler** (July 24, 1861–February 16, 1919), that he was going to West Texas to seek his fortune and he would come back and marry her. He wasn't gone very long when recurring visions of the girl at the well convinced him to turn around and come back to Gainesville. He promised his future father-in-law that he would always treat Mary nicely, be true to her, work hard and make a good living. He lived up to that promise until the flu epidemic of 1919 claimed his wife.

Gus Meyer became a respected stonemason in Gainesville. Much of the yellowish native stone he used for building foundations and curbing in Gainesville's downtown area came from a quarry just east of Gainesville, north of the KGAF radio station location. The stone foundations of some of those brick buildings, which are over one hundred years old, are a testament to Gus Meyer's craftsmanship.

Meyer also got a contract to lay brick streets in Gainesville before the Katy Railroad connected Gainesville to Denison. He purchased five large Studebaker wagons to haul brick from Denison. It was a two-and-a-half-day trip counting the time to load and unload.

In making his run from Gainesville to Denison and back, Gus hauled a variety of things in addition to bricks. He commonly traded information with the mail riders on the same road. On one of his trips, a mail rider overtook Gus's wagons on the way to Gainesville. Gus made the mistake of telling the mail rider who was traveling faster than he was that one of his wagons had dresses from Paris, France, and to inform the people that he was two hours out from Gainesville. When he and his wagons got close to town, he could tell there was a big cloud of dust around a cluster of trees on the edge of town. He told his men to approach with caution in case of Indians or some kind of marauders. The cloud of dust was caused by an excited bunch of women who had come out in their buggies, anxiously awaiting the latest Paris fashions. Gus vowed never again to tell mail riders what he was hauling.

Toward the end of Gus Meyer's life, this ninety-three-year-old man who literally helped build Gainesville had his patriotism to the United States called into question because of World War II. All residents of the United States who were born in either Germany or Japan came under special scrutiny. He received an order by mail to bring any radios he owned to the courthouse for inspection. Gainesville's "man of stone" did his duty and turned his tabletop radio in at the courthouse. He was notified three weeks later to come pick up his radio. He walked with his cane from his house to the courthouse to claim his radio and walked back home with the radio under one arm and his cane in the other. His daughter and grandson, H.K. Lyde, met him a short distance from home. With tears in his eyes and pointing to the radio, Gus Meyer exclaimed, "See, they know I'm a good American!"

In a sense, Gus Meyer took his craft with him. Six massive stones completely encase Gus and Mary Meyers' burial plot, which is twelve by twenty-four feet. (MAP: GM)

Killed by a Pot of Beans

Johnnie Ruth Kammerdiener (July 28, 1939–March 3, 1942), daughter of **John E.** (b. June 9, 1902) and **Sally A. Kammerdiener** (November 25, 1900–August 20, 1959), died as a result of turning over a pot of beans cooking on the stove. She was scalded by the beans and also suffered burns from the flames on the stove. The Kammerdieners resided at 345 North Morris Street, Gainesville. (MAP: JK)

Division 18

People of Color

Former Slave Centenarian

Bob Scott (August 10, 1825–February 3, 1926), a former slave, was probably the oldest resident of Cooke County when he died at the age of one hundred. Those in the white community called him "Uncle Bob." He fit the "Uncle Tom" stereotype of the kind of black man who was obedient and subservient to white authority. According to his death notice in the *Gainesville Register*, "Uncle Bob" didn't spend much time with "colored folks." "I has six months to attend to my own affairs, and six months to leave other people alone every year."

Bob was born into slavery in Tennessee. As a young adult, he was sold to William Scott by Bill Barrett, a Tennessee slave trader. William Scott brought Bob to Gainesville ten years later, when Gainesville had only four residences.

William Scott passed Bob on to his son, Rufus. Bob Scott lived with the Colonel Rufe Scott family for many years on East Scott Street. He slept in the house while the colonel was away during the Civil War, ready to protect Mrs. Scott and the children with an axe if necessary. During the "Great Hanging" tragedy, he drove the wagon carrying the condemned to their fate on Pecan Creek.

For a ten-year period after the war, he hauled corn from Pauls Valley to Fort Sill, Indian Territory. Much of his working years were spent farming. **Sarah Scott**, Bob's wife, preceded him in death on January 19, 1917, at

Bob Scott, former slave, lived to be one hundred years old. He drove the hanging wagon of many of the victims of the "Great Hanging of 1862." *Taken from* Gainesville Register *microfilm, Cooke County Library*.

the age of seventy-one. Reserved seating was set aside for white mourners at Bob Scott's funeral at the St. James CME Church. Scott's former owner, **Rufus Scott**, is buried in Division 2. (MAP: SC)

RESPECTED WATER ENGINEER DIED OF FOOD POISONING

Powell Johnson (d. March 19, 1892) and his wife (name and burial place unknown) both died of food poisoning, probably from eating tainted sausage, as that was the only food found in the house at the time of their deaths. Powell's wife's death occurred the day before his. The *Hesperian* speculated on the day of his death: "At this writing Powell is not conscious and is breathing fast. He cannot last much longer."

The *Hesperian* praised Powell's work as an engineer at the city waterworks, where he had been employed for several years. Prior to that, he had been a well-respected engineer at a cotton mill in Alabama. "A more honest faithful man could not be found," and he had friends "among white people as well as people of his own race." (MAP: PJ)

Namesake for Moffett Park

Ned Moffett Sr. (1842–November 9, 1924) was a mulatto farmer (as described by the 1880 census) who owned ninety acres of land on the west side of Elm Creek on the outskirts of Gainesville. He and his wife, Mary Stone Moffett, were married on April 19, 1866. This marriage resulted in five boys and four girls.

Moffett allowed the black community to use his property near the creek for picnics and special celebrations. After his wife's death in 1931, the heirs gradually sold the Moffett acreage. Two sales totaling approximately five acres to the City of Gainesville in 1943 resulted in a "Negro Park" in Gainesville, later to be called "Moffett Park." The first big celebration in this city park occurred appropriately on Juneteenth Day of 1944. This was a racially segregated park until 1966. (MAP: MO)

Two of Moffett's Children Drowned in Separate Incidents

Clint L. Moffett (February 16, 1872–October 12, 1920), the forty-eight-year-old son of Ned Moffett, was found drowned in a water well at the Moffetts' home west of Elm Creek. He had been deaf for many years and lived with his parents.

Lula Hill (1878–March 9, 1952), the seventy-four-year-old daughter of Ned Moffett, was also found drowned in a well at the home of Mary Johnson, 1005 Muller Street. She had been missing for almost one week after disappearing from the home of her nephew, Moffet Rawlston, at 811 Potter Street in Gainesville. Justice of the Peace Clyde J. Matherly ruled accidental death, although the box surrounding the well was approximately four feet in height. The decomposition of the body made it difficult to conduct a postmortem examination. Both children are buried near Ned Moffett. (MAP: MO)

UNKNOWINGLY CAUSED CHILDREN TO BEHAVE

Catherine "Aunt Kate" Greenwood (d. October 28, 1939), approximately one hundred years old, was found dead in her home on West Carnes. She was one of the founders of the AME Methodist Church at the corner of Scott and Weaver Streets. She was known as "Aunt Kate" to both the black and white communities. Her funeral was held at her home.

In her latter years, she was a mysterious-looking old woman, commonly seen carrying a tow sack on the streets of Gainesville. The tow sack contained coal that she had gathered along the railroad tracks and kindling that she picked up around Gainesville. The *Weekly Gainesville Register* described how she was unknowingly used to scare children into behaving:

> *To countless Gainesville children in their tender years, she was an unwittingly enigma and supposedly had some supernatural powers for punishing those who disobeyed their parents. Many a fond mother and father, unable to control their youngsters had threatened "to call Aunt Kate" who would take them away in her sack, as the parents pictured it. It is unlikely that the aged negress knew she was being used as a disciplinarian in such manner, but the ruse usually worked.*

(MAP: CG)

GRANDMOTHER WHO RAISED RENOWNED CHICAGO CONCERT SINGER

There was no notice printed in the newspaper when **Mary Houston** died and was buried on April 4, 1941. In those days, Negroes were rarely mentioned in the newspaper unless they were accused of a crime. However, Mary Houston's grandson, Theodore Charles Stone, was acknowledged in the *Register* not because he was here for his grandmother's funeral but because he performed a selection of songs before the Gainesville Kiwanis Club. Theodore's parents, Samuel William and Rosa Houston Stone, died when Theodore was a young boy, so he was raised by Mary Houston, his maternal grandmother.

As a boy, Theodore did odd jobs for **Maggie Vaeth** (Division 20). She, in turn, gave him music lessons. After graduating from Booker T. Washington in Gainesville, Theodore attended Huston-Tillotson College in Austin. There he continued to develop as a baritone singer and moved to Chicago in 1932 to study at Chicago Musical College (now a division of Roosevelt University).

He was encouraged to go to Finland to study by Kosti Vehanen, accompanist for Marian Anderson. Stone was the first black student to attend the Sibelius Academy in Helsinki, Finland. He became fluent in French, Italian, Finnish and Swedish. The outbreak of World War II forced him back home. Stone's musical repertoire included opera, Finnish folk tunes and Negro spirituals. He performed to wide acclaim in Chicago, Pittsburgh, St. Louis, Cleveland, St. Paul and Gainesville. In 1945, he performed a benefit for St. James Colored Methodist Episcopal Church at Booker T. Washington School.

Theodore Charles Stone also became a music critic for various newspapers. For a number of years, he was president of both the Chicago Music Association and the National Association of Negro Musicians. He died October 17, 1998. His papers—which include photographs, musical programs and sheet music of black composers—are in the Center for Black Music Research at Columbia College, Chicago. His brother, **Samuel Stone** (1902–January 3, 1978), is in Division 23. Sources of information on Theodore Charles Stone include the websites of the National Association of Negro Musicians and the Center for Black Music Research. (MAP: MH)

A Black Doctor with Integrated Practice, Charged Based on Ability to Pay

Dr. Oregon F. Strong (August 15, 1888–January 1, 1961) was the first black doctor in this area. His mother and father and family came to Gainesville from Mississippi in 1889. His mother was a teacher, and his father had been a college professor.

After receiving his degree from Meharry Medical College in Nashville, Tennessee, Oregon began a medical practice out of his office in the front of his house on the southwest corner of Scott and Weaver Streets. The back of his house served as the "colored" funeral home.

His patients were blacks and whites of all levels of the economic spectrum, although he was known as the cheapest doctor in town. The patient could pay off his bill at the rate of fifty cents a week or with foodstuff during harvest season.

According to *Black History as Remembered by Black Gainesvilleites*, Dr. Strong charged $1.25 for a house call, $3.00 to deliver a baby and $3.00 for a tonsillectomy. According to a former patient, Dr. Strong also had a well-deserved reputation for the treatment of syphilis, which he probably acquired due to a bawdy house in his neighborhood.

For many years, Dr. Strong did not have local hospital privileges. He commonly performed surgery on a patient's kitchen table under kerosene lamps. Sheets might be boiled in water with lye soap on a wood stove. Chloroform was the anesthetic. Later, when black patients were allowed to be treated at the Gainesville Sanitarium, Dr. Strong attended them in the basement of the hospital among the heating and plumbing pipes.

Dr. Strong died from complications of diabetes some time after the amputation of a leg. (MAP: OS)

Division 18A

His Brother and Barbed Wire Lured Him to Texas

Charles C. Sanborn (December 10, 1837–December 24, 1923) was born in Jay, Vermont. He followed his more famous younger brother, Henry B., to Texas and settled in Gainesville about 1886 to open a feed, seed and hardware store at the corner of Chestnut and California. Streets. One of his featured products was "Glidden No. 5" barbed wire, which his brother had introduced to Texas and Gainesville in September 1875. Charles was a competitor of **Cleaves** (Division 4) and Fletcher Hardware, which was probably the first dealer of this barbed wire in Texas. What these three entrepreneurs had in common is they were all Yankees in origin. Charles's brother, Henry, developed a model ranch in western Grayson County, later created the "Frying Pan Ranch" in West Texas, and became the "Father of Amarillo."

Charles was survived by his wife, **Elizabeth Leonard Sanborn** (November 10, 1839–May 26, 1924); daughter, **Corinne (Mrs. Edward M.) Patchell** (March 30, 1868–March 28, 1944); and son, **Charles Lee Sanborn** (August 7, 1871–February 3, 1936). Sanborn's funeral, as was the custom in large homes, was conducted in his home on South Denton Street. His granddaughter, **Mary Patchell** (May 5, 1892–December 5, 1976), was a longtime English teacher in Gainesville High School and Gainesville Junior College. (MAP: SA)

Popular Saloonkeeper

John Stice (d. July 8, 1905), a "popular California Street saloon man," died suddenly at his home of apparent heart failure. His saloon was the Board of Trade.

Coincidentally, in the same column of the *Daily Hesperian* announcing his death, there was an article announcing a temperance lecture to be given by Reverend John Carney of Weatherford the coming Sunday on the courthouse square. The title of the talk was "The Saloon Must Go." There was a movement at the time to vote Cooke County "dry." (MAP: JS)

Spanish Influenza Claimed This Soldier

Leon Jirasek (1899–October 12, 1918) died of Spanish flu at Fort Sill, Oklahoma, where he was stationed. He was one of the thousands of the victims of the worldwide flu epidemic during World War I. His uncle, **Frank Jirasek** (Division 6A), had adopted his orphaned nephew. Leon's funeral was conducted at his uncle's home. Leon had volunteered in July. He was a baker by trade, and that was his job at Fort Sill. (MAP: LJ)

Unsuccessful Republican Candidate for Lieutenant Governor

J.L. (Jerra) Hickson (August 20, 1859–March 3, 1929) was a staunch Republican in Gainesville when he was definitely in the minority. **A. Morton Smith** (Division O) in *The First 100 Years in Cooke County* repeated a story about an incident involving J.L. Hickson, who reported the ongoing results of the 1884 presidential election between James G. Blaine, the Republican, and Grover Cleveland, the Democratic winner. Hickson posted the election returns on a blackboard in his bookstore on California Street. The Democrats who gathered there got mad when they heard the rumor that the Studebaker Company had threatened to fire any worker who voted for Cleveland. A mob of local Democrats stormed a warehouse, stole a Studebaker wagon and burned it with a straw effigy in the wagon on the courthouse square.

In 1906, during Hickson's first term as Gainesville postmaster, an impressive new post office was built on the corner of Denton and California Streets. Prior to this time, the post office had functioned in rented buildings.

In 1916, Hickson was an unsuccessful Republican candidate for lieutenant governor of Texas. Democratic voters in Cooke County outnumbered Republican voters by about seven to one in those days. (MAP: JH)

Division 19

F.M. Dougherty: Frontier Lawmaker and Entrepreneur THM

F.M. (Francis Marion) Dougherty (February 13, 1826–December 27, 1895) was a dominant figure in the formative years of Gainesville, and his monument dominates the landscape of Fairview Cemetery.

Although Dougherty's father was a cotton planter in Mississippi, Francis Marion—evidently named for the American Revolutionary War hero—was born in Florence, Alabama, in 1826. He came to Texas seeking his fortune in 1844, settling in Hopkins County, working first on a cattle ranch and later getting experience as a store clerk there. When he moved to McKinney, he became successful in the mercantile business and served one term in the Texas House of Representatives from 1855 to 1856.

After marrying **Lou Armstrong Huffman** (1832–1885) in McKinney, the newlyweds moved to Gainesville, and Dougherty continued successfully in the mercantile business. In 1861, the Cooke County Commissioners Court appointed Dougherty to be a captain of the local militia. Later, he was elected captain of Company A of the Sixteenth Texas Cavalry (dismounted) in the army of the Confederacy. He fought in the Battles of Mansfield, Pleasant Hill and Jenkins Ferry.

Dougherty was elected to the Texas House of Representatives in 1879 and reelected in 1881. The legislature in 1879 faced a number of varied problems, including an empty treasury, a dispute with Oklahoma over the possession of Greer County, the cost of building a new capitol, the cost of frontier defense against Indian attacks, boundary problems between counties and the definition of a lawful fence. To help meet the state deficit, the legislature repealed the 1876 law providing for annual pensions for surviving soldiers and signers of the Texas Declaration of Independence and their widows.

Due largely to the already serious financial burdens of the state, Dougherty was a member of a five-member minority on the House Finance Committee who voted against the state's purchase of the Alamo at a proposed cost of 112,000 acres of land. Dougherty declared, "The Alamo's value as a historic landmark does not depend on its ownership and preservation by the state…its possession by the state will entail a heavy outlay at the outset and a constant demand ever afterwards upon the state treasury for its preservation, upon the slender hope that such a course will strengthen patriotic feelings."

Dougherty voted with a majority of the members of the legislature to give Texans a little tax relief. The legislature repealed a one-dollar tax on dogs that had been enacted in 1876. A hydrophobia problem had prompted that earlier tax on dogs, which exempted one dog per household.

Of immense local interest to Representative Dougherty was the legislation to better define the Cooke County–Montague County line. The resulting legislation authorized any county court to appoint "an experienced and practical surveyor" to make county lines well defined. Survey markers were to be posts, earthen mounds or stone markers. Posts were to be of hewn cedar, cypress or bois d'arc, at least eight inches in diameter, five feet long and set at least three feet in the ground. Earthen mounds or stones had to be a minimum of two feet high. These markers were to be placed in one-mile intervals. Field notes were to be filed in the county clerk's office, and copies were to be filed with the General Land Office.

There was also significant debate concerning the legislature's definition of a "lawful fence" as mandated by the new state constitution. Dougherty presented a minority report against the proposal to require a plank of at least five inches wide and one inch thick along the top of a barbed wire fence. Dougherty argued against this proposal because of the huge expense to farmers having to comply with this standard. The legislature spent a significant amount of time fine-tuning fence legislation during this period.

In 1881, one of Dougherty's losing votes was over who the legislature would elect as United States senator from Texas. Sam Bell Maxey, ex-

Confederate general from Paris, was elected. Dougherty cast his vote for James W. Throckmorton, who was briefly governor after the Civil War until removed by the United States government. Throckmorton Street in Gainesville is probably named for this ex-governor.

In addition to his role as lawmaker, Dougherty was part of the economic elite of Gainesville. He was president of the First National Bank, which opened for business on the northeast corner of the courthouse square on January 1, 1883. In 1887, he became president of Gainesville Compress and Warehouse Company and, later still, president of the Gainesville Board of Trade, which was organized to promote the Gainesville-area economy in the post–cattle boom years. His work on the board of trade in 1891 resulted in the creation of a county fair on a forty-acre plot on the corner of Broadway and Fair Avenue.

F.M. Dougherty died at his home on December 27, 1895. His funeral procession to the cemetery included 112 vehicles. He was preceded in death by his wife, Lou, ten years earlier. He was survived by one son and two daughters: **William H. Dougherty**, Cora M. Fairchild and Frances M. Houston. The Lou Dougherty Chapter of the United Daughters of the Confederacy was organized and named in his wife's honor about 1900 and was responsible for the Confederate soldier statue in Leonard Park, erected in 1908.

Much of this narrative was originally part of the application process for a Texas Historical Marker. (MAP: DO)

The Man Responsible for the "Washington Monument"

William H. (Holmes) Dougherty (1857–February 7, 1924) was a very successful cattleman and banker, following in the footsteps of his father. When the Atchison, Topeka and Santa Fe extended its rail line from Gainesville up into Indian Territory in 1887, Henderson Flat took on a new importance as a cattle-shipping point and was renamed "Dougherty" for William. Later, he acquired over 2,700 acres of land in Floyd County, Texas, and became a stockholder in the Floyd County Lumber Company. In 1928, his influence in Floyd County led to the naming of a new town in southeastern Floyd County "Dougherty" for his father, **F.M. Dougherty.**

William and his wife, **E.N.** (d. April 30, 1933), donated their home to the city, and it served as the main Gainesville High School building for approximately four decades. Dougherty also made his mark on higher education by serving as a member of the board of regents for the University of Texas.

Dougherty was also responsible for commemorating his family with the landmark monument of Fairview, which is a fifty-foot-tall obelisk, apparently an imitation of the Washington Monument.

According to Joe Carroll of George J. Carroll and Son Funeral Home and James Richards, whose family has been in the monument business since 1899, William Dougherty purchased this monument in the late 1800s in Chicago, where it was "some kind of historical marker." After some research, I am convinced that this monument came from the Columbian Exposition of 1893, the Chicago World's Fair. Many objects of that fair were sold at its

Looking east toward the Dougherty obelisk, the dominant architectural feature of Fairview Cemetery. This monument probably came from the Chicago World's Fair of 1893.

conclusion. An 1896 article in the *Scientific American* entitled "The Fate of the Chicago World Fair's Buildings" mentions an obelisk near the south lagoon of the fairgrounds and also declares that there are "'bits' of the World Fair all over the world." The Santa Fe Railroad office in Gainesville offered special excursion fares during the fair. The Dougherty monument, I believe, is a Texas-size souvenir of that World's Fair. (MAP: DO)

A New High School in Gainesville

Shortly after the death of **Isaac Newsome Dougherty** (1893–February 19, 1920), son of William H. and E.N. Dougherty, his parents volunteered to give their three-story mansion on South Lindsay Street to the City of Gainesville to be the high school of the city, provided the city name the high school "Newsome Dougherty Memorial High School." For a little over half a century this impressive brick building was the high school for Gainesville, whose students claimed "NDMHS" stood for "Nine Darn Months of Hard Study."

The Dougherty mansion was formerly the home of **Senator Joseph Weldon Bailey** (Division 21). The third floor of this building was the birthplace of North Central Texas College (originally Gainesville Junior College) in 1924. (MAP: DO)

Brigadier General CSA

William Hudson (1829–March 11, 1904) played a central role in the defense of Gainesville in the "Great Hanging" of 1862 and during the Civil War. The Cooke County Commissioners Court, of which he was a member in 1861, authorized the creation of two companies of volunteers with the appropriation of $1,200. One of those companies was headed by Captain W.C. Twitty, and the other was headed by Hudson. Later, as military commander in Gainesville, Hudson was responsible for assigning Newton Chance to act as spy to infiltrate the "Peace Party," which led to the "Great Hanging."

Hudson was born in Randolph County, Alabama. From Alabama, he originally settled for a few years in Rusk County, Texas, arriving in Gainesville in 1854. After the war, he was a partner with **J.M. Lindsay** (Division 8) in the land business until 1883. In his later years, he was a partner with his son, **Walter Sr.**, in a stock farm on Spring Creek.

General Hudson died in the home of daughter **May**, **Mrs. F.A. Tyler** (Division 21). The *Gainesville Register* invoked these sentiments: "In his death Gainesville loses another landmark."

Hudson was a charter member of the Cumberland Presbyterian Church and a charter member of the first Masonic lodge in Cooke County, #210, A.F. and A.M. He was buried with full Masonic rites, and his pallbearers consisted of the Gainesville elite: **William H. Dougherty**, **W.O. Davis**, **J.M. Lindsay**, **D.L. Painter and George Y. Bird.** According to the *Gainesville Register*, a female chorus sang his three favorite hymns at the funeral: "Asleep in Jesus," "Lead Kindly Light" and "Abide with Me." (MAP: WH)

From Drover to Millionaire: J.D. "Ikard" Sugg THM

J.D. (Joseph D.) "Ikard" Sugg (1854–August 10, 1925), on his own at the age of thirteen, became a cowboy by the age of fifteen. His story is indeed a Horatio Alger kind of story. By the time of his death in 1925, his wealth from cattle, land, banking and other investments was approximately $10 million.

Born in Mississippi, he was the youngest of three children. The family moved to Arkansas when he was four years old. His father, T.C. "Tom" Sugg, and brothers fought for the Confederacy. In 1867, after his mother died, J.D. walked alone to Camden, Missouri, where he survived financially by stemming tobacco.

In 1868, he continued his trek. He walked across Arkansas, through Indian Territory to Red River, north of Gainesville. He spent the night on a ferry in the middle of Red River to escape being "eaten up" by mosquitoes. Penniless, he traded his bandana for a breakfast of corn cakes, bacon and coffee.

Not long after arriving in Texas, J.D. latched on to a cattle drive going from South Texas to Wyoming. He started as a wrangler's helper, and after several cattle drives from Texas to Wyoming, he became boss of herds going the same route. Sugg acquired enough money to buy his own herd from his cattle drive earnings and from shooting buffalo. In 1875, his older brother, **Eli Calvin** (1850–July 7, 1902), joined him, and they began a cattle ranching operation on Mud Creek in Indian Territory with the backing of Gainesville banker **William H. Dougherty**. Shortly after, they were joined by their father, a former plantation owner and Mississippi River boat captain. Another brother, John, and his wife, Narcissa, moved nearby.

Their ranch, the IS Ranch, was located on the Chisholm Trail and eventually grew to cover a large area, bounded by Beaver Creek and Cow Creek between the town of Waurika and Red River. J.M. Dyer in his *History of Jefferson County, Oklahoma*, states that the Suggs "were pioneers and wore the name well." The Sugg brothers were friends of neighboring rancher Burk Burnett and Quanah Parker. Because of their lease of Comanche land, the Suggs had a good relationship with Quanah Parker. Quanah and his tribesmen had the habit of coming to the Sugg ranch in the fall to gather pecans to sell, and the Suggs provided them with beef while they were there.

The town of Sugden, south of Waurika, developed as a result of the Suggs' ranching operations. It reached its heyday in the 1890s. By 1899, it had a hotel, general store, cotton gin, blacksmith shop and Presbyterian church. Its decline started when it lost in the competition with Waurika to be the county seat of Jefferson County.

S.H. Woods was a cowboy for the Suggs in the spring and summers for six years, beginning in 1881. In *The Trail Drivers of Texas*, he recalled his first cattle drive for the Suggs in 1881. This sixteen-year-old was "second boss" of a drive from Monument Hills, just north of the Sugg ranch headquarters, to the vicinity of Big Horn Mountain, Wyoming. That drive of three thousand yearlings went via Dodge City and Ogallala to Powder River, Wyoming, and from there up the Crazy Woman River to their Wyoming headquarters.

In 1882, the Suggs' ranching enterprise spread to northern Donley County, north of Clarendon, Texas. The Sugg brothers became partners with J.W. Sacra. The Suggs used the Bar O brand on this ranch. About 1888, Charles Goodnight purchased the Sacra-Sugg Ranch to expand his cattle empire.

The Suggs continued to be involved in cattle drives to Wyoming. The Texas Trail Monument in Goshen County, Wyoming, lists the Suggs' Bar O brand next to Charles Goodnight's JA brand.

About 1898, the Suggs were having trouble with their grazing privileges on Comanche lands shortly before the land rush of 1901. Consequently, the

Suggs moved their ranching enterprise to the San Angelo area. They bought the Triangle N Ranch and the 7-D Ranch there. Suggs, Texas, southwest of San Angelo in the southwestern corner of Irion County, was named for the Suggs because of their OH Ranch there. J.D. Sugg also had a separate ranch near Sherwood. The Suggs' ranches shipped cattle to Fort Worth, and the government of Mexico was a major buyer of their horses.

About 1912, J.D. moved to Chickasha and became involved in a frenzy of economic development there. In 1913, he built a new building for the First National Bank, as president of that bank, and also built the Sugg Theatre. He also built cattle pens on the north side of Chickasha.

J.D. Sugg waited too long to seek treatment for stomach cancer at the Mayo Clinic, and he died at his home, 802 South Eighth Street, in Chickasha on August 10, 1925. Sugg's estate and his generosity were impressive. His real estate holdings in Grady County, Oklahoma, were valued at $872,000. His Texas estate included 280,000 acres in Irion, Reagan and Sterling Counties; a 10,000-acre ranch in Tom Green County; another 16,000-acre ranch in Irion County; and stock in the San Angelo streetcar line. He also had investments in banks, an insurance company and an oil company.

Sugg left **William H. Dougherty** $25,000 to benefit the Cooke County poor farm and $5,000 to go toward the maintenance of Fairview Cemetery. He forgave one farmer's mortgage and left him $5,000. When one of J.D. Sugg's ranches was liquidated in 1927, it resulted in the roundup, sale and delivery of one thousand horses to the government of Mexico.

J.D. Sugg and his brother **Eli Calvin** illustrate the transformation from itinerate cowboys to respected ranchers. J.D. Sugg, in particular, is a personal example of the successful transition from the "Old West" to the "New West."

This essay was originally part of the application for a Texas Historical Marker. (MAP: SU)

HAD A SECRET FAMILY

Eli Calvin Sugg (1850–July 7, 1902), **Ikard Sugg's** older brother, was a partner of his in the ranching business. According to Gwen Jackson in *Indians, Cowboys and Homesteaders*, Cal and Ikard promised each other not to marry. In the 1890s, Cal was seeing a schoolteacher in Indian Territory, and then she mysteriously disappeared. Years later, when Cal was gravely ill in the hospital in Gainesville, Ikard learned that Cal had married that schoolteacher. That schoolteacher, **Luette Clement Sugg** (1866–September 5, 1907), is buried in Fairview with her husband. Cal's secret family lived in Clearmont, California. Luette had three children: Calvin H., Andrew A. and a daughter who was killed in a car accident near Ardmore.

In 1910, when Ikard filed some papers concerning his brother's estate in probate court in Gainesville, Ikard declared that Cal (in the cowboy tradition) had no fixed domicile "but spent much of his time in Cooke County and claimed the same as his domicile." Cal had died of stomach cancer in the home of **William Dougherty**. According to the *Dallas News*, Cal owned the Comer and J.B. Wilson ranches in Irion County, and they were the largest in that section of Texas. (MAP: SU)

First Lumberyard in Gainesville

D.L. (David) Painter (1827–1911), a native of Virginia who migrated to Gainesville via St. Louis, established the first lumberyard in Gainesville in 1870 at the future site of the Lindsay Hotel. Lumber was hauled by wagon prior to the coming of the railroad from his supplier in Denison, the Waples-Lingo Company. In 1875, Painter and Paul Waples formed the Waples-Painter Company. In 1903, **J.D. Leeper** (Division 19) replaced Painter as president of the company.

In 1904, Painter sold a twenty-acre tract on the east side of Elm Creek where the city had built a dam to become a city park. For several years the park was called Painter Park. Later, it became known simply as City Park until the 1920s, when it officially became Leonard Park, named for former mayor **John T. Leonard** (Division 19) due to his campaign to beautify the park and build a pavilion there. (MAP: DP)

Owner of First Hotel in Texas with a Phone in Every Room

Luther D. Turner (June 29, 1877–June 20, 1952) was a civic leader and longtime owner and operator of Gainesville's premier hotel, the Turner Hotel, on the north side of California Street just west of the Santa Fe

Depot. He followed his father, **David H. Turner** (Division 14), in the hotel business. Luther joined his father's business in 1902 after returning from school in St. Louis. On November 21, 1907, he married **Fay Painter** (d. August 23, 1969), daughter of **D.L. Painter**.

For many years, Luther and his brother **Edgar** (Division 14) shared leadership of the hotel company until Edgar's death in 1941, when Luther became sole head of the company. In 1927, they built a six-story brick hotel with a ballroom on the top floor. It was the pride of Gainesville and was reportedly the first hotel in Texas with a telephone in every room. The hotel company was left in the hands of Luther's two sons, **William C.** (Division 22) and David P. Turner, at his death.

Throughout his life, Turner was very active in civic affairs and activities that promoted the city of Gainesville. During World War I, he was home service chair of the American Red Cross. Under his leadership, Turner Field, a landing strip with a refreshment cottage off South Weaver Street just north of the current city sewer treatment plant, was developed. The committee had an agreement with U.S. Army Air Corps training officials at Caruthers, Hicks and Barron Fields in Fort Worth to provide this field for cross-country flyer training. According to Morton Smith's *First 100 Years*, from 1917 through 1918, the field handled ten to fifteen flights daily, and on some Sundays there were as many as fifty planes on the field. When flyer **Ed Sullivan** had his fatal crash in Ardmore after flying from Turner Field, Luther brought his body back and was in charge of his funeral arrangements.

Turner was in charge of transportation arrangements for the Gainesville Community Circus in its early years and, in later years, was a promoter of local athletic clubs, especially baseball. His civic endeavors included serving on the Gainesville city council and the Gainesville school board. (MAP: LT)

Watchmaker, Jeweler, Bicyclist

William B. Kinne (April 28, 1866–December 9, 1945), when he was a boy, moved from Wisconsin to Gainesville. He studied watchmaking with several local watchmakers prior to establishing his own jewelry store. That store remained under his family's control for about a century and continues today under the Wiese family ownership at 210 East California Street. It contains a museum that perpetuates the Kinne family history.

In 1890, Kinne organized and served as drum major of a marching band, which performed at the county fair, German celebrations and Confederate veteran reunions. Kinne was also a local leader of the bicycling craze of the 1890s. He was elected president of the Gainesville Bicycle Club and donated a gold badge to first place in the one-mile bicycle race in Gainesville on July 4, 1896. According to Morton Smith, bicycles became such a nuisance that the city enacted a city ordinance in 1897, requiring them to be equipped with a light and a bell for the safety of pedestrians and buggy drivers. (MAP: WK)

Carriage and Spur Manufacturer

George A. Bischoff (October 16, 1861–May 17, 1944) had a varied career as a manufacturer of carriages and spurs and later a dealer in horseless carriages. He was born in Emmettsburg, Maryland, in a family of ten children. He completed an apprenticeship at Baker Carriage Company and began his carriage making in Dallas. While visiting his parents in San Antonio, Florida, he met his future wife, **Mollie Jane Tucker** (August 18, 1868–October 15, 1954) of Dade City, Florida.

In 1894, he moved to Gainesville, where he operated G.A. Bischoff Carriage Works on the corner of Main and Rusk Streets across from city hall. His company also did blacksmithing work, and when J.R. McChesney took his spur manufacturing company to Pauls Valley, Oklahoma, Bischoff filled the void by hiring a former McChesney employee, Albert C. Dickerman, to continue the manufacturing of spurs.

When Bischoff learned that former President Teddy Roosevelt was coming to the Fort Worth Stock Show in 1913, he decided he needed an appropriate pair of spurs and gave that job to Dickerman. The spurs featured "eagle head shanks with diamond eyes and silver rowels" in a gold mounting, Dickerman later recalled in the *Register*.

From 1906 until 1912, Bischoff served on the Gainesville city council and, according to the *Register*, was instrumental in converting the water system in Gainesville from private to public ownership. He was grand marshal of the Gainesville Labor Day parade in 1913.

Bischoff owned the first Maxwell automobile in Gainesville and for a while had the Maxwell dealership. In 1910, he and W.L. Greenhill became partners in operating the Overland automobile dealership.

Bischoff left Gainesville in 1916, moving to Kansas City, and again in 1926 to Oklahoma City. He made the news after the beginning of World War II by working as an accomplished dyemaker for Douglas Aircraft despite his advanced age.

His funeral was in St. Joseph's Cathedral in Oklahoma City with full Knights of Columbus rites. Prior to burial by Leazer-Keel Funeral Home, his body laid in state at the home of his daughter, Mrs. J.W. Schad, at 946 North Commerce Street. (MAP: GB)

Pioneer Newspaper Publisher

John T. Leonard (September 30, 1848–August 9, 1935) died of heat prostration shortly after driving around in the city park that bears his name, Leonard Park. His name was synonymous with the *Gainesville Register* for over forty years.

He was born and lived in Shepardsville, Kentucky, until he was sixteen, when he moved to Illinois, where he met his wife, **Mary Elliott** (1855–December 6, 1924), of Oconee, Illinois. They came to Gainesville in 1885. His first occupation in this area was schoolteacher. As a teacher at Fair Plains school in southern Cooke County, he became a correspondent for the *Weekly Hesperian*. His journalistic skills earned him the job as editor of the *Hesperian*.

His son, **Joe Means** (Division K), who was named for Leonard's boss at the *Hesperian*, was born in 1890, the same year his father purchased the *Gainesville Register*. Leonard, as mayor from 1901 until 1910, spearheaded city park improvements, street paving and the construction of a new central fire station among his accomplishments.

Leonard's wife, Mary, as a pedestrian, was fatally struck by a car in front of the *Register* offices in 1924. (MAP: JL)

Nationally Known Epilepsy Specialist

Dr. Jerry Clay Price (February 24, 1904–September 24, 1950) was a nationally known epilepsy specialist who died in Los Angeles of carcinoma. He was the son of **Norine "Nora" Wooldridge Price** (February 24, 1875–February 28, 1948) and **Dr. William James Price** (January 19,

1861–October 2, 1927). Jerry grew up in Gainesville and was a graduate of Vanderbilt University and Tulane University School of Medicine. He practiced medicine in Gainesville for a number of years. From 1934 to 1936, he was vice-president of the Gainesville Community Circus. In 1936, he was elected president of the Cooke County Medical Association.

He left Gainesville to do advance medical study in Boston, and from there he went to New York City to become a research associate at the Neurological Institute of Columbia University, which was the first specialty hospital in the United States to study disorders of the nervous system exclusively. Price was a co-founder of a national association to control epilepsy. His medical practice was in Los Angeles at the time of his death. He was survived by his wife, Jane, and stepson, Tommy.

This eternally young little girl marks the grave of Margaret Mary Price, deceased in 1900. She endures all seasons next to her brother, Dr. Jerry C. Price.

A statue of an innocent little girl is adjacent to the Jerry Price grave. It represents his baby sister, **Margaret Mary Price** (February 7, 1899–January 15, 1900). (MAP: JP)

Received a Pension for Husband's Service in the Texas War for Independence

Martha E. Conlee (August 6, 1834–November 20, 1924) survived her husband, **Preston Conlee** (Division 4), by a little more than fifty years. She was considerably younger than her husband, since she was born in 1834 in Louisiana and came to Texas in 1848, twelve years after Texas gained its independence from Mexico. Her application for a pension on July 16, 1883, is a link to her husband and his military service in the Texas War for Independence. Under an act of the Texas legislature of March 28, 1883, she was entitled to a government pension. That document also mentions that she received a veteran donation land certificate for 1,280 acres. She is buried in the plot of her daughter, **Sue McKemie**. She also had three other daughters and a son, Preston Conlee of Ardmore. (MAP: MC)

A Family of Two Legislators and a "Nightingale"

Dixie Valeria Potter (May 23, 1862–May 21, 1934) is buried with her father, **Thomas J. Crooks** (1833–April 3, 1909), and her husband, **C.L. (Calhoun "Coon" Landers) Potter** (March 6, 1854–April 29, 1905). Crooks, formerly of Denison, was a state representative in the Eighth Texas Legislature in 1863, representing the Eleventh District, which included Gainesville.

C.L. Potter was a prominent Gainesville attorney who was a state senator in the Twenty-second, Twenty-sixth and Twenty-seventh legislatures in 1891, 1899 and 1901, respectively. As a six-year-old boy, he and his parents moved to the Marysville area in northwest Cooke County near Fish Creek from Pontotoc County, Mississippi, via a one-year stint in Grayson County. When he was eight years old, Indians burned the family home while he and the Potter and Landers women were hiding in the woods. Subsequently, his family moved to Whitesboro, where they resided for several years until they moved back to Marysville.

He left Marysville at nineteen to study law with his older brother, Gainesville attorney **Clement Clay Potter** (Division 4). After one year of study, he became a law partner with his brother, and that partnership endured until C.L.'s death in 1905, except for the interlude when C.C. was district judge.

In 1876, he married **Nellie Walton** (April 18, 1859–December 10, 1885). She is buried next to her infant along with her father-in-law and mother-in-law, **Cincinnatus Potter** (January 24, 1822–October 18, 1898) and **Melissa A. Potter** (January 23, 1826–January 31, 1883), in Division 9. Nellie and C.L. were survived by two daughters, Mrs. Walton Harris of South McAlester and Edith Potter of Gainesville.

Prior to her marriage to C.L. in 1887, Dixie Crooks of Denison "was a concert singer of prominence, known as 'the Texas nightingale,'" according to the *Gainesville Register*. After her marriage, for a number of years she was soloist and choir director of First Methodist Church in Gainesville. In public appearances, one of her most frequently requested songs was, appropriately, "Dixie." As an elderly widow, she moved to Denver to be close to her son, James. As a pedestrian, she was the fifty-third traffic fatality for Denver in 1934 just shy of her seventy-second birthday.

According to the *Fort Worth Record*, C.L. narrowly missed being the Democratic nominee for lieutenant governor at the 1892 Democratic State Convention. The nomination required a two-thirds vote, and Potter was eleven votes short. The paper claimed Potter's chance at the nomination was due to an unfounded rumor that he was not loyal enough to Governor Jim Hogg. (MAP: PO)

Founders of Valley View

Lawrence Washington Lee (October 27, 1831–February 12, 1916) and his wife, **Mary Ann (Fryer) Lee** (January 16, 1840–November 7, 1934), were the founders of Valley View. They were married on November 1, 1859, at Prairie Home in Cooper County, Missouri. They came to the future site of Valley View by oxcart on February 1, 1870. With a ten-year-old daughter, **Ella Lee**, they were leading a group of families, primarily from Cooper and Johnson Counties in Missouri.

The site they picked was a true wilderness with grass as high as a man's head. Mrs. Lee is attributed with naming the town site "Valley View" because of the view looking west. Lee offered every family a lot to build on, providing each would paint its house white. On March 26, 1872, Valley View was granted a post office.

Lee is commonly referred to as "Captain Lee." This was not a military title but probably a title in reference to two cattle drives he commanded from Missouri to California or because of his being in command of the group of families coming from Missouri to Texas. This information is courtesy of Norman Newton of Valley View. The Potter-Hurley home, a recorded Texas Historic Landmark, on Church Street in Gainesville, was built in 1894 as a wedding gift from Captain and Mrs. Potter to their daughter, **Ella Lee Potter** (Mrs. J.M. Potter) (December 28, 1860–April 26, 1933), also buried in Division 19. (MAP: LL)

Registered Over Two Thousand Women to Vote in the Democratic Primary, 1918

Parx O. Hays (March 23, 1876–December 2, 1949) was county tax collector from 1917 to 1921. In 1917, the Texas legislature passed a law that allowed for the voter registration of women for the 1918 Democratic primary prior to the approval of the Nineteenth "Women Suffrage" Amendment in 1920. Women, unlike men, did not have to pay a poll tax for the privilege of voting. The registration period for women for the Democratic primary on July 27 was from June 26 through July 12. Women could register at the tax office at the courthouse or in their homes if they notified the tax collector. Parx Hays went all over the county following a definite schedule and registered many women in their homes. His office registered over two thousand women during the registration period.

He and his wife, **Ianna J. Hays** (May 29, 1880–February 14, 1972), were the parents of **Margaret Parx Hays** (Division 24), Gainesville's first female mayor. (MAP: HA)

The "Ins and Out" of the Hughes Mausoleum

The **Hughes** family mausoleum, across the street from the **Dougherty** family obelisk, was constructed in 1925. This double-domed structure was once an impressive, open edifice, but it has been sealed for years and is in a deteriorating condition. The tale of this structure involves three generations of Dr. Hugheses: **Dr. C.T. Hughes** (September 14, 1860–January 15, 1942), **Dr. Roy E. Hughes** (1888–July 12, 1925) and Dr. Roy Gene Hughes of Kingsland, Georgia.

The patriarch of the family, C.T. Hughes was a native of Alabama. He graduated from Alabama State Teachers College in Florence and spent some time in Texas teaching before he decided to go to medical school. He attended the University of Alabama Medical School, where he met his future wife, **Darline Earle** (March 3, 1864–May 5, 1961). After marriage and C.T.'s graduation from Louisville, Kentucky School of Medicine, the couple came to Texas, settling briefly in Meridian and then Houston. They came to Gainesville in 1898 to escape the Houston climate.

According to Morton Smith's *First 100 Years*, Dr. Hughes had the distinction of buying the first automobile owned in Gainesville. It was a 1903, one-

Students of North Central Texas College in front of the Hughes mausoleum, experiencing the "cemetery as classroom."

cylinder Oldsmobile he bought for his fifteen-year-old son, Roy. Through a *Dallas News* ad, the horseless carriage was bought from a McKinney banker. However, two men who were driving the vehicle to Gainesville got stalled somehow in Valley View, and they had to hire two horses to pull it the rest of the way in the middle of the night. Roy's driving frightened horses and mules whose owners on the streets of Gainesville would commonly shout, "Stop that thing!"

Young Dr. Roy Hughes, who practiced medicine with his father, lost his wife, **Midge Hay** (d. December 16, 1924), "following a short illness," according to the *Register*. Her death, however, was probably from difficulty with a pregnancy, since cemetery records reveal that she was buried with an infant. Her survivors included two small children, **Helen Hay "Patsy,"** six years, and Roy Eugene, five years.

A little over six months later, Roy was tragically killed while learning how to fly in a new plane he had owned for two weeks. He and his flying instructor, James B. Cole, an ex-army pilot, took off from a dirt strip on the Hughes place south of Gainesville, headed for Dallas. After about six minutes in the air, a witness saw a puff of smoke come from the plane. It crashed on the Davis farm south of Elm Creek. Cole either jumped or was thrown from the plane and escaped with cuts and bruises. Roy burned to death, strapped in his seat. After his funeral, Gibson Funeral Home housed his body until the completion of the Hughes mausoleum.

Darline Hughes lived to be ninety-seven years old. The latter part of her life she lived with a daughter, Mrs. L.A. MacArthur Sr., of Theodore, Alabama. After her death in a Mobile hospital, she was placed in the mausoleum.

Now the strange end to the story: **Helen Hay "Patsy" Guerdrum** (March 17, 1918–Deember. 1, 1968), daughter of Midge and Roy Hughes, died in Washington, D.C. According to local resident Marge Powell, Patsy's brother Dr. Roy Gene Hughes considered her the "black sheep" of the family and had the mausoleum sealed, refusing to allow his sister to be placed inside. She is buried in front of the mausoleum. Her friends reportedly took up a collection to pay for her grave marker. (MAP: HU)

Grandparents of Lieutenant Governor Bob Bullock

Sallie Rebecca Mitchell (1855–July 10, 1930) and **Thomas Douglas Mitchell Sr.** (1857–February 24, 1921) were the parents of Mrs. T.A. (Ruth) Mitchell Bullock, mother of Bob Bullock, dominant Texas political figure who was comptroller of public accounts and subsequently lieutenant governor in the 1980s and 1990s. In a letter to Cooke County Judge Russell Duncan in declining an invitation to speak at the dedication of the Texas State Historical Marker for Fairview Cemetery in October 1997, Bullock recalled that his grandparents "were affectionately known as 'Papa Grande' and 'Mama Grande.'" (Incidentally, the restoration of the Texas State Cemetery in Austin was a pet project of Bullock's at the end of his political career.)

T.D. Mitchell was a well-respected traveling representative of some large manufacturing firms for over two decades. He was fatally stricken with a heart attack while waiting in Uvalde for a train to bring him back to Gainesville. His funeral, held in his home on South Denton Street, was well attended by the Gainesville elite. Trinity Patrick Lodge No. 7 of the Knights of Pythias conducted the graveside service.

Sallie Rebecca Mitchell died in Waco almost a decade later. The Bullock family was living in Hillsboro at the time. (MAP: MI)

Namesake for Football Stadium

James D. "J.D." Leeper (1862–May 7, 1936) was a pioneer in the lumber business. He and his brother, Graves, founded Leeper Brothers Lumber Company about 1879. Their business grew rapidly. In addition to the lumberyard on Chestnut Street in Gainesville, they had locations in Denison, Decatur and Bowie. When the Santa Fe line was extended from Gainesville into Indian Territory, Leeper Lumber located at several points along that line in Indian Territory.

In 1890, Leeper was a co-founder with R.D Gribble, C.C. Hemming, W.W. Howeth and others of the Hesperian Building and Savings Association. It was a unique financial institution and had a longevity of almost one hundred years.

In 1925, Leeper donated land to the city for a high school football stadium behind Newsome Dougherty Memorial High School. That stadium, Leeper Stadium, was for many years the home of the Gainesville Leopards and, briefly in the late 1920s, home of the Gainesville Junior College Tigers. The last high school football game was played there in 2009, prior to the construction of a new high school and stadium adjacent to I-35. (MAP: LE)

FOUNDER OF XLI WOMEN'S CLUB

Nettie C. (Mrs. J.D.) Leeper (1864–September 11, 1940) organized the first women's literary and civic club in Gainesville in 1893. It was called the XLI Club because it was limited to forty-one charter members originally. It was patterned after the XXI Club in Denison. Nettie had attended a meeting of that club and was inspired to create a similar club. The nucleus of that club attended a Thanksgiving dinner meeting at the Leeper home that featured a speaker from the Denison club.

Over approximately fifty years, the XLI Club hosted literary events and organized civic activities. It donated four hundred books to the first city library in 1903. The club initiated the movement to erect a memorial clock in the dome of the courthouse to memorialize those from Cooke County who died in the Great War, World War I. This was accomplished in 1920. In 1939, a book club, originally called the "Junior XLI Club," was a spinoff of the original club.

Nettie also founded Associated Charities in 1905 and was active in this forerunner to the United Way for thirty-five years. Its primary function was providing food, clothing and fuel to the needy. (MAP: LE)

CIVIC LEADER AND "CONSCIENCE OF GAINESVILLE"

Leannora "Nora"Hudson Rose (May, 14, 1869–April 3, 1953), a prominent progressive reformer, died after a lengthy illness at the age of eighty-three. She was a descendant of two prominent pioneer families of Cooke County. Her father was **General William Hudson** (Division 19), and her grandfather was **Wilson L. Fletcher** (Division 4), owner of the first hotel in Gainesville. A formally educated woman, she graduated from

Ward Seminary in Nashville, Tennessee, in 1887. Throughout her life, she lived a short distance from her birthplace at Church and Commerce Streets, residing at 321 South Dixon.

In 1891, she married a native of Fredericksburg, Virginia, **Robert Selden Rose** (February 8, 1856–January 18, 1952). He was actively involved in the cotton brokerage business for many years until his retirement in 1936.

Nora was a charter member of the XLI Club and a charter member of the Bible Presbyterian Church. She was elected the first chairwoman of the Cooke County Red Cross in 1917 and was heavily involved in wartime endeavors of that organization. As a prominent member of Associated Charities, she was instrumental in selecting the beneficiaries of that charity.

In 1935, she tried to goad the white people of Gainesville to improve school facilities for blacks in Gainesville. She wrote a newspaper article entitled "Our Forgotten People." That article stimulated a group of white women to approach the Rotary Club to become an ally to get a new school for blacks. The women were told to be patient; a movement was afoot to build a new junior high and a new school for blacks. The campaign started for a new junior high, but nothing was said about a new school for blacks.

In a letter to the *Register* in May 1936, Nora continued her campaign for a new school for blacks. She reminded the readers that in 1935 the *Register* "spoke of the disgrace of letting our children attend such a dark and incommodious building," referring to the junior high. "Never a word about the more disgraceful, unsanitary, dark building the negroes have used for over 40 years." The current building for blacks, she declared, had been condemned. (Blacks got a new school, Booker T. Washington, a 1938 WPA project.)

Nora Rose castigated the local hypocrisy. "All of this talk about planting shrubs and sweet-smelling flowers to show off for the [Texas] Centennial tourists makes me sick when I know of the stench in our city's backyard." Moreover, she added, many southern churches were building modern schools in Mexico, Brazil, China, Japan, Korea and Africa.

Nora Rose was persistent in her diligence to make Gainesville a better place. (MAP: NR)

Division 20

Pioneer Buffalo Hide Dealer

Alonzo Wasson (March 23, 1846–February 4, 1920) and his wife, **Sarah Jane (Tealy)** (1848–January 1929), with baby Alonzo, moved from Fort Smith, Arkansas, to Sherman in 1871. Wasson was born in New York but was raised in St. Louis. In Sherman, he became a dealer in wool and animal hides, which was a lucrative business for a number of years. According to the *Register*, "His business grew to such extent that he is said to have bought the hide of practically every buffalo that was killed on the western plains." After "business reverses," he moved to Gainesville in 1882, where he was in the insurance business.

His son, Alonzo, became a prominent journalist as editor-in-chief of the *Dallas Morning News* from 1920 until 1929. He began his journalism career at the *Register* in 1891. He worked for several other newspapers until he was hired by the *Dallas News* in 1905 as a Washington correspondent. (MAP: AW)

Last of the Confederate Veterans

D.T. Lacy (April 1, 1846–March 17, 1942), a ninety-five year-old pioneer banker who died in 1942, was the last of the Cooke County Confederate veterans.

Son of Donald Ross and Jane Bailey Lacy, he was born in Madison County, Tennessee, but his family moved to East Texas when he was a boy. He joined the Confederate army in Henderson, Texas, in December 1863. As a seventeen-year-old enlistee, he served as a messenger and never was actually involved in combat. D.T. Lacy received his discharge from the army in Marshall when the war ended.

After studying commercial business in New Orleans, he migrated to Gainesville in 1880. According to the *Register*, he was a founder and one of the original stockholders in the First National Bank in Gainesville when it was organized in 1882. His bank was at the center of the financial "wheeling and dealing" during the cattle boom of the 1880s. From 1890 until 1904, he was its vice-president, and from 1904 until its merger with Lindsay National Bank in 1930, he was bank president. He officially retired after the bank's reorganization in 1933 as Gainesville National, although he still retained an office in the bank that he frequented until two days before his death.

In 1939, he moved from his two-story residence at 904 North Weaver to 522 South Morris in Gainesville. He donated his Weaver residence to St. Mary's School to serve as its high school. He was a lifelong bachelor and was survived by two nieces, Mrs. R.F. Jackson and Miss Eva Noble. (MAP: DL)

FIRST AMONG HIS "PEERS"?

John Valentine "Val" Peers (1861–October 22, 1918), a well-respected, retired businessman, died in his room at the home of Mrs. Hines on Cravens Street. Val Peers had suffered from sciatic rheumatism along with Bright's disease for the past fifteen years. He was survived by two daughters: Mrs. Merlin Mitchell of Gainesville and Katherine Peers, who was in New York City preparing for Red Cross work in France at the time of Val's death.

Peers was born in Farmington, Missouri, and came to Gainesville about 1883. He operated the Tennessee store here for many years and was involved in other businesses later. "In his early business career he was very successful and amassed a considerable fortune, but later misfortune and bad luck swept away most of his substance. He remained a warm and genial person." His wife was the former **Allie O'Hara** (1872–June 16, 1914) of Sherman. She committed suicide by ingesting carbolic acid.

Val Peers was at the top of his class in every school or college he attended. According to the *Register*, "He was an incessant reader and one of the best posted [i e., informed] men in the country. His private library is said to be one of the best in North Texas." (MAP: VP)

Music Teacher of Renowned Black Concert Singer

Maggie Dean Peurifoy Vaeth (March 16, 1867–January 4, 1934), native of South Carolina and wife of German emigrant **Francis Otto Vaeth** (January 22, 1863–November 4, 1939), was a brave woman, giving a black teenage boy piano lessons in her home in the mid- to late 1920s. It was probably their secret, since this was shortly after the Ku Klux Klan was openly active in Cooke County with the county attorney, Fred Wankan, as its public leader. Theodore Stone, a student at Booker T. Washington School, did odd jobs for Mrs. Vaeth, and when he showed an interest in the classical music he was exposed to in her home, she started giving him piano lessons. Stone eventually became an internationally famous baritone singer as a resident of Chicago. During World War II, the Gainesville ladies' XLI Club sponsored him in concert.

This information is from the *Register* and the website of the Chicago Music Association. (MAP: VA)

Another Railroad Casualty

Hopkins S. Cassady (October 12, 1881–August 8, 1913), brakeman for the Missouri, Kansas and Texas (the Katy) Railroad, was killed in a freight train wreck near Denton. His death is another reminder of the dangerous nature of working for the railroad.

Cassady's wife, **Emma Kleuser Cassady,** sued the railroad for liability in her husband's death. She won her suit in district court in Gainesville. The Katy appealed the decision to the court of appeals in Fort Worth. The railroad lost in that court and unsuccessfully appealed to the Texas Supreme

Court. According to the *Gainesville Register*, Emma won for herself and her three minor children a "big damage" claim amounting to $18,500 after a two-and-a-half-year legal battle. She was represented by the local law firm of Stuart, Bell and Moore. (MAP: CA)

An Indulgent Mother

Emma Kleuser Cassady (1884–1938) was born in Montrose, Missouri. According to Vern Bivin in *Cooke County History*, "She was a beautiful brunette, a fashionable dresser, and a canny businesswoman" who owned the Lyric Theater on the west side of the courthouse square. She was an indulgent mother to her two sons, George S., born in 1907, and Emmett Buckner, born in 1909. In 1927, under intense lobbying from her sons, she bought them a World War I Canuck-type training plane. She hired Wiley Post to teach them to fly. Two years later, she bought them a Travelair OX-5 biplane. After barnstorming for a while and operating Red River Flying Service, they both became military pilots. In 1932, George was part of the first graduating class of what became the "West Point of the Air" at Randolph Field, Texas.

Both boys had distinguished military careers during and after World War II, rising to the rank of brigadier general and major general, respectively. George, who was killed in a car wreck in 1966, is the only non-Indian buried in the Maricopa Indian Cemetery in Arizona. A propeller from an OX-5 marks his grave.

One of the sources of information for this entry was the website of the U.S. Air Force. (MAP: CA)

Division 21

Commander of Local GAR

In light of the "Great Hanging" of 1862, it is remarkable that **Henry E. Schopmeyer** (1837–1909), a former Yankee soldier in the Civil War, was elected to the Gainesville City Council during the 1880s, serving one of his several terms with former Confederate general **William Hudson** (Division 19).

In the decade of the 1890s, Schopmeyer played in the Gainesville band organized by **W.B. Kinne** (Division 19). Schopmeyer also was commander of the Samuel R. Curtis Post #12 of the Grand Army of the Republic, the organization of Union veterans of the Civil War. Schopmeyer Street in Gainesville is a reminder of his influence in Gainesville in the late nineteenth century. (MAP: HS)

Comrade W.H. Garmany CSA

W.H. Garmany (July 1, 1840–September 13, 1920), in addition to being a founder of a Christian Science society in Gainesville in 1911 and serving as Gainesville city treasurer from 1912 to 1920, had a unique story in connection with his service in the Confederacy. The following is a memorial resolution written by a committee of the Joseph E. Johnston Camp 119 of the United Confederate Veterans honoring its longtime adjutant:

Comrade Garmany was born in Rome, Georgia, July 1, 1840, and was 21 years old when he volunteered for service in the Confederate Army December 13, 1861. He belonged to Company K, 55th Alabama Infantry, Scott's Brigade, Loring's Division, Army of Tennessee. John T. Stewart of Goshen was his captain.

Comrade Garmany was not in any of the early battles of the war, on account of his health. He was in various hospitals at times until his illness became so severe he was taken to a private home—that of a Mrs. Odneal—where he was cared for until he became convalescent. He was then put in the Ordinance department, but on account of the condition of his lungs, his physicians ordered him to return to his command with a recommendation that he be discharged. The command was in action almost continually so it was some weeks before he reached it, and by this time his condition was so improved he reported for duty—not discharge.

This was reported in the *Gainesville Weekly Register*, August 18, 1921. (MAP: GA)

PROMINENT BUSINESSMAN, CONFEDERATE VET

F.A. Tyler Jr. (1848–April 3, 1919) was a prominent grocery wholesaler for many years with his partner, John L. Simpson. Tyler preceded Simpson to Gainesville by one year, arriving in 1878. Their friendly competition to supply groceries to Santa Fe construction crews extending the railroad to Gainesville led to their partnership. In 1888, the *Gainesville Hesperian* reported that this dominant North Texas grocery partnership was "controlling the trade from Gainesville north to the Canadian River on the Santa Fe, and west on the Missouri Pacific and Fort Worth and Denver to Quanah in the panhandle, beside the large wagon trade." They moved into a giant warehouse on the west side of the railroad tracks on the south side of California Street in 1889. In 1890, Tyler was a charter member of the Gainesville Board of Trade, the forerunner of the chamber of commerce. Eventually, F.A.'s son, William H., took his father's place in the business in 1917, and the company had branches in Ardmore, Duncan, Pauls Valley, Norman and Fort Worth. (The building is now an antique mall.)

Tyler was a Confederate veteran, and his grave is marked with the only Confederate iron cross in Fairview. This is the "Southern Cross of Honor" with a Confederate battle flag surrounded by a laurel wreath at its center on one side. On the reverse side is the phrase "Deo Vindice," which means "[With] God [as our] Vindicator," with the years 1861–1865. This emblem was originally a medal authorized by the Congress of the Confederacy on October 13, 1862, for "loyal service to the South," the Confederate equivalent to the Union's Medal of Honor. Beginning from a Confederate veterans' reunion in 1898, the United Daughters of the Confederacy authorized this emblem to be bestowed on any Confederate veteran who gave "loyal, honorable service to the South." The United States Veterans Administration authorizes the use of this emblem on grave markers for Confederate veterans. (MAP: TY)

"Fatty," the Beer Man

L.A. "Fatty" Fleenor (October 6, 1866–December 25, 1910) has his nickname, "Fatty," prominently displayed on his ornate tombstone along with the Odd Fellows symbol, the three-link chain. He moved to Gainesville from Era shortly after his marriage on February 22, 1891, to **Rose** (May 9, 1868–March 7, 1953), who was a native of Illinois. Until April 1896, he owned and operated the Star Restaurant at 215 East California Street, which he sold to Sing Lung when he became the Anheuser-Busch distributor.

Anheuser-Busch had a brewery in Gainesville and bragged about selling twice as much beer as its leading competitor until Gainesville voted "dry." On election day on August 8, 1903, the "drys," demonstrating in downtown Gainesville, chanted, "'Fatty' Fleenor is coming off the [beer] wagon!" The "drys" defeated the "wets" by a margin of approximately 200 votes out of a total of approximately 2,500 votes countywide.

A Fleenor infant is buried with Fatty and Rose. That tombstone features the common lamb, symbolizing innocence, and bears the poignant inscription:

Earth has one mortal less
Heaven one angel more.

(MAP: FF)

HER SHOE LED TO HER IDENTITY AS ACCIDENT VICTIM

Bertie Lee Woods Parks (June 11, 1893–April 26, 1923), resident of Wichita Falls and formerly of Gainesville, was killed in a car wreck involving an intercity Dallas–Fort Worth taxi in which she was a passenger and a truck stalled on the Dallas–Fort Worth Pike near Mountain Creek. She was thrown through the windshield and rendered unconscious. Her purse with her identification was lost or stolen, so her identity was unknown when she reached St. Paul's Sanitarium. Hospital personnel, after some effort, identified her by phoning a shoe store whose name and Wichita Falls address were printed inside one of her shoes. The hospital gave the shoe store a physical description of her over the phone, and because she was a regular customer of theirs, they could identify her.

Bertie Lee's family, including her husband, Pierce Parks, a railroad conductor who was in Denver at the time of the accident, and her sister, Mrs. Oral Blake of Gainesville, were at her bedside when she died, never regaining consciousness, three days after the accident. The *Register* obituary intoned: "It is hard to realize that Bertie Lee is dead, for she was just plain Bertie Lee to those of us whose good fortune it had been to number ourselves among her circle of friends."

Her body was brought to Gainesville by the Katy Railroad and lay in state at the home of her sister at 223 North Denton Street prior to the funeral at St. Paul's Episcopal Church. (MAP: BP)

SHERIFF'S DEPUTY SURVIVED WORLD WAR I TO BE KILLED BY A TURKEY THIEF

William Warner Emerson (January 19, 1887–December 5, 1927) was born in Borren County, Kentucky, and he and his parents moved to the rural areas of Montague and Cooke Counties when he was a young boy. He was one of the first volunteers to enlist in the Gainesville Machine Gun Company in the 142nd Infantry in the 36th Division for World War I. He fought in France and achieved the rank of first sergeant, returning without being wounded.

Because of his war experience and reputation as a peerless leader, Sheriff **Jake Wright** (Division 21) hired Emerson as his chief deputy. The arrest

On the left is Sheriff Jake Wright (Division 21); on the right is Deputy William Emerson, World War I veteran, killed by a turkey thief in 1927. *Taken from* Gainesville Register *microfilm, Cooke County Library.*

of a suspected turkey and chicken thief turned deadly for the deputy with slightly less than one year's experience on the job.

Tenant farmer Claude Autrey filed a complaint at the sheriff's office regarding the theft of some of his turkeys and chickens late at night. He accused a neighbor, Dave Wilson. When Autrey identified some of his stolen fowl on the Wilson farm southeast of Gainesville, Sheriff Wright and Deputy Emerson returned with a search warrant. They rousted Wilson out of bed about 7:00 a.m. and had him put on his clothes and meet them in front of his house. After Wilson came outside, he told the sheriff he needed his hat because it was so cold. Both the sheriff and deputy were wearing overcoats, which interfered in the ensuing struggle with Wilson.

When Wilson slammed the door going back into his house, Sheriff Wright suspected something and immediately followed him in. Wilson waved a revolver at the sheriff, and the sheriff lunged at the suspect. In the violent struggle, Wilson beat the sheriff repeatedly on the head with the handle of his gun, which proved to be unloaded. Deputy Emerson came to the aid of the sheriff, and they dragged Wilson outside while he continued to struggle.

After the deputy had Wilson subdued, holding him from behind, he asked Autrey, who was standing by, to find something to tie up Wilson. Autrey found some clothesline wire, but tragically, the deputy refused it because it would cut up his suspect. While waiting for some rope, Wilson reached into the deputy's overcoat pocket, pulled out his .45 revolver and shot the deputy. Deputy Emerson, sensing what was coming, crouched down. The bullet pierced his lower abdomen and exited the back side of his thigh. According to court testimony, Wilson yelled for Emerson to shoot him when he regained his gun. But he refused and holstered his gun. The wound was not immediately fatal, but Emerson died the next day in the Gainesville sanitarium because of complications from a blood clot that entered his lung.

According to the *Gainesville Register* account, Wilson was not kept for long in the Cooke County jail for fear of its lack of security—he might escape—so he was transferred to a more modern jail, the Tarrant County jail in Fort Worth. The local jail was good enough for Wilson's wife, who was indicted for turkey theft. Dave Wilson, twenty-eight, prior to this incident, had had one brush with the law over a dance hall he had operated in the Woodbine community. He was sentenced to ninety-nine years in the penitentiary by the Sixteenth District Court in the Cooke County Courthouse in February 1928 for Emerson's death. (MAP:WE)

PROGRESSIVE STATE REPRESENTATIVE

W.L. (William Lafayette) Blanton (December 28, 1851–May 27, 1937) died two days after being struck by a car on the corner of California and North Commerce Streets in Gainesville. He had a distinguished career as attorney, city attorney and two-term member of the Texas House of Representatives (1905 and 1907). As a progressive lawmaker, he was co-author of banking legislation and author of the Blanton Pure Food Act in 1907.

Blanton was born in Unionville, Tennessee, and attended Unionville Academy there prior to moving to Gainesville. He was a three-term city attorney from 1880 to 1886. In 1886, W.L. married **Sarah Allen** (1857–1905), whose grave is marked with a square column adorned with a pensive female figure in Division 4.

In 1896 he was grand master of Texas Odd Fellows and, according to the *Gainesville Register*, was a trustee for both the Odd Fellows' Orphans Home and the State School for Boys in Gatesville.

He was survived by his second wife, **Gertrude Burns Blanton** (1872–March 31, 1961), whom he married in Galveston in 1908. They had a twenty-one-year age difference. (MAP: WB)

Joseph Weldon Bailey: Sam Rayburn's Boyhood Idol THM

Joseph Weldon Bailey (October 6, 1863–April 13, 1929) was the dominant political figure in Texas between the Jim Hogg era and the "Pa" and "Ma" Ferguson era. Bailey served five terms in the United States House

United States Senator Joseph Weldon Bailey (1863–1929). To many, he was a hero; to W.O. Davis and others, he was a scoundrel. Bailey said he could not join the church because he would have to forgive W.O. Davis. *Courtesy of Morton Museum of Cooke County.*

of Representatives (1891–1901) and two terms in the United States Senate (1901–13). For the brief highlights of this man, read his Official Texas Historical Grave Marker. The following is adapted from the essay used to justify his historic marker.

Joe Bailey was the son of Joe and Harriet (Dees) Bailey, born near Crystal Springs in Copiah County, Mississippi, on October 6, 1863. As a student debater at the University of Mississippi, he was in awe of United States Senator Lucius Quintus Lamar. He later imitated Senator Lamar's antebellum style of dress early in his own political career. That style of dress was rather long hair, broad-brim hat and long Prince Albert coat.

At the age of twenty-two, after graduating from the Cumberland (Tennessee) Law School, Bailey followed his future wife, **Ellen Murray**, to Texas. He became the law partner of C.B. Stewart of Gainesville. Bailey once remarked: "Gainesville is the best town in the world in which to live but the hardest in which to make a living."

Within his first year of living in Gainesville, Bailey gained local attention by delivering an oration on the courthouse square honoring the recently deceased Ulysses S. Grant. He used his oratorical skill to defeat an elderly incumbent to the United States House of Representatives and became the youngest member of the House.

Bailey's oratorical skill was commonly compared favorably to William Jennings Bryan. Fannin County teenager Sam Rayburn rode a horse twelve miles to Bonham to hear Congressman Bailey speak.

When the House of Representatives convened in 1897, Bailey was elected House Democratic minority leader. He was part of the congressional leadership that pushed President McKinley to war with Spain. However, after the Spanish-American War, Bailey and William Jennings Bryan both became critics of American imperialism and were opposed to keeping the Philippines.

The subtitle of Sam Hanna Acheson's biography of Senator Bailey is *The Last Democrat*. Acheson is referring to the Jeffersonian kind of Democrat with belief in limited government. Bailey's stand against American imperialism was based on the Jeffersonian principle of the right of the people to govern themselves:

> *A republic in the nature of things is incapable of dealing with colonial possessions...If there is any one principle dearer to all others to a genuine,*

> *old fashioned democrat: it is the right of local self government and I am utterly unable to understand how any disciple of Jefferson can support the policy which violated the cardinal principle he taught.*

In 1900, Bailey decided to move up to the United States Senate. His popularity and oratory proved too much for the incumbent, Senator Horace Chilton, who withdrew from the race. This Senate campaign and the one in 1906 were prior to the Seventeenth Amendment (1913), which gave people the power to directly elect their United States senators. Bailey was elected to his two terms in the Senate by the Texas legislature.

An action by the United States Supreme Court on March 17, 1900, would eventually result in a scandal involving Senator Bailey. The Supreme Court upheld the Texas Antitrust Act and the Texas attorney general's decision to take away the Waters-Pierce Company's charter to do business in Texas. The attorney general's action was based on the idea that the Waters-Pierce Company was a subsidiary of Standard Oil, in violation of the Texas Antitrust Act.

According to Bailey's chief biographer, Bailey met H. Clay Pierce, the chief executive officer of the Waters-Pierce Company, in St. Louis on his way back to Washington. Pierce wanted to hire Bailey as his company's attorney. Bailey told Pierce he didn't need an attorney if he obeyed the law.

At that time, Joe Bailey was having financial difficulties. He had bought six thousand acres of land in Dallas County and invested in a horse farm in Kentucky. (Bailey was a horse lover and had his own horse track west of Gainesville.) Bailey signed a personal note with Pierce for $3,300. Later, Bailey talked to the governor and attorney general, and a new Waters-Pierce Company was given permission to do business in Texas.

Public rumors surfaced about Bailey's relationship with the Waters-Pierce Company. In January 1901, the Texas House of Representatives voted to investigate the relicensing of the company to determine if there was any impropriety involved. Bailey testified he had not accepted a legal fee from the Waters-Pierce Company but failed to mention the personal loan he had received from Pierce. By a House vote of 87 to 25, Bailey was exonerated. On the same day, the Texas legislature overwhelmingly elected him to the United States Senate by a vote of 110 to 4.

In addition to financial problems, Bailey had an extreme temper that was never more apparent than on June 30, 1902, when he made national headlines. After a verbal skirmish on the floor of the Senate with Senator Albert Beveridge of Indiana, Senator Bailey attempted to choke Senator Beveridge while he sat at his desk right after the Senate recessed. What provoked this assault was that Bailey had criticized a friend of the Indiana senator, and Beveridge had responded by calling Bailey's remarks an "unwarranted attack."

The high-water mark of Joe Bailey's oratory was in defense of a strong Interstate Commerce Commission as a tough regulator of railroads. To that end, he spoke extemporaneously for four hours and ten minutes to a packed Senate gallery. The *New York Daily Tribune* called his speech one of the best heard in the Senate since the Civil War. Bailey declared that if a strong Hepburn Act regulating railroads were passed, "we would hear no more of railroad senators and railroad politics."

A July 1906 issue of *Cosmopolitan Magazine*, the muckraking publication of William Randolph Hearst, featured Joseph Weldon Bailey in its fifth installment of a series entitled "Treason in the Senate." This article renewed the controversy about Bailey and his relationship with the Waters-Pierce Company and triggered another investigation by the Texas House of Representatives. He was exonerated again after a five-week investigation in early 1907, and the Texas legislature reelected him to the Senate.

Bailey didn't mince words in talking about his enemies. He accused them of being "Populists, infidel Republicans, and Socialists," and he also claimed, "We are going to bury them face down, so that the harder they scratch to get out, the deeper they will go toward their eternal resting place." Furthermore, he speculated that if the people of Texas got tired of him, he could be elected to the United States Senate by the new state of Oklahoma. Bailey's opponents also had strong words for him. One suggested, "Bailey is too pretty to be a man, too fat to be a woman, and too oily for us."

Bailey vociferously disapproved of two movements that were in a sense products of World War I: national prohibition and women's suffrage. He argued that liquor regulation should be a police power of the states. He also believed women were incapable of the "three highest duties of citizenship": serving in the military, aiding in law enforcement and serving on juries. In a 1913 letter, Bailey expressed the opinion that men had already made almost all bad habits a crime and women would be radical reformers who would make bad manners a crime.

Finally, in 1920, Bailey decided to fight against the "evils" of progressivism by running for the governorship of Texas in the Democratic primary. He had three progressive opponents: B.F. Looney, R. Ewing Thomason (also from Cooke County) and Pat Neff. Bailey received a plurality of the votes in the first primary because the progressive vote was split. Bailey was defeated in the runoff primary by Pat Neff, and Bailey even failed to carry his hometown of Gainesville.

Shortly after his defeat, Bailey moved his law practice from Washington to Dallas. Although he specialized in civil law, one of his more noteworthy clients was Dr. Frederick Cooke of Fort Worth, a former Arctic explorer who was convicted in federal court of fraudulent oil stock selling. Bailey died of a heart attack while representing a Red River bridge company in the Fifteenth District Court in Sherman on April 13, 1929.

Joseph Weldon Bailey, this complex political giant, was buried two days later in the most elaborate funeral ceremony ever witnessed in Cooke County. A charter train brought mourners from Dallas. Schools and businesses were closed. Former Chief Justice of the Texas Supreme Court Nelson Phillips

Unloading Senator Bailey's casket for graveside service on April 15, 1929. A plane flown by Gainesville's Cassady brothers dropped flowers on his grave. *Courtesy of George J. Carroll & Son Funeral Home.*

delivered a brief eulogy. The Gainesville Chamber of Commerce arranged for local aviators, the Cassady brothers, to drop flowers from their low-flying plane on Bailey's grave.

The Cross Timbers Genealogical Society's *Fairview Cemetery* erroneously says that Joseph Weldon Bailey's body was moved to Dallas. It was Bailey Jr.'s body that was moved.

Ellen Murray Bailey (d. Oct. 23, 1926), wife of Joseph Weldon Bailey for over thirty years, had the reputation of a genial hostess in Washington during Joe Bailey's years in Congress. Her health declined after their move to Dallas in 1920. She died at their residence, 3008 Maple Avenue, Dallas. She and her husband had two sons, Joe Weldon Jr. and Weldon of Tucson, Arizona. The family members came from Dallas to Gainesville to her funeral in the private railroad car of the president of the Texas and Pacific Railroad.

Joe Bailey remarried on December 21, 1927. His second wife was Prudence Rosengren of Austin. (MAP: JB)

MOTHER AND SISTER HAD A PREMONITION ABOUT THE DEATH OF THIS SOLDIER

First Lieutenant James Arthur Manahan (June 9, 1889–September 12, 1918) was killed in World War I at Fey en Hey, France. The night he was killed, according to the *Register*, **Anna Manahan** (November 28, 1851–August 5, 1947), his mother, dreamed at first that she was shot in the forehead and then realized it was her son who was shot in the forehead. That same night, Lieutenant Manahan's sister dreamed that he was standing by her bed and he said, "Don't worry, May, I have been given a decent burial."

A letter Mrs. Manahan later received from Lieutenant Olenbush confirmed that Lieutenant Manahan was killed instantly from a machine gun bullet to the forehead and that the chaplain had given him a decent burial.

Lieutenant Manahan was born in Temple but grew up in Gainesville. He was working in a drugstore in Wichita Falls when he decided to enlist on May 9, 1917. He received his officer training in San Antonio and was shipped to Europe in June 1918. His body made its trip home approximately three years later.

On that Sunday afternoon, August 14, 1921, much of Gainesville turned out to line the streets to witness one of the most dramatic funeral processions in Gainesville history. The pallbearers carried the flag-draped casket from the church to the caisson, flanked on both sides by uniformed soldiers. A twenty-piece chamber of commerce band led the four-horse caisson, followed by comrades in arms, followed by other mourners. Reverend E.M. Dunsworth, who presided over the funeral at Grand Avenue Baptist Church, told of Lieutenant Manahan buying a home for his parents shortly before going to Europe.

An estimated crowd of three thousand witnessed the graveside service conducted by the local American Legion post, led by Commander Gilbert Holman. The Honorable George H. Culp and the Honorable R.E. Thomason delivered patriotic remarks at the graveside. Boy Scouts were used for crowd control at the cemetery. After a three-shot salute, a bugler played "Taps" near the grave, and another bugler in the distance played "Taps" as an echo effect.

The face of Lieutenant Manahan's tombstone features an American flag and identifies him as "1st Lt. Co. C 357 Inf 90 Div., Killed in action near Fey en Hey, France during St. Mihiel Drive." The back side of his tombstone offers this poem:

Brave boy was he
He went to his country's call.
And yet we do not forget,
Many a brave boy had to fall.

(MAP: MA)

Two Generations, Two Wars

Lieutenant Manahan's father, **J.R. (James Randolf) Manahan** (January 13, 1847–May 29, 1927), buried near his son, was a Confederate veteran. J.R. was born near Aberdeen, Mississippi, and at the age of fifteen took his father's place in the Confederate army. He fought at Vicksburg as a private in Company G, Thirty-first Mississippi Regiment (the same regiment in which **Judge J.P. Hall**, Division 14, served), Featherstone's Brigade, Loring's Division, Stewart's Corps, according to the *Gainesville Register*.

He married **Anna Isabella Alsup** on October 6, 1869, and they moved shortly after that to Fort Worth. They moved to Gainesville in 1910. J.R. was the commander of the Joseph E. Johnston United Confederate Veterans Camp at the time of his son's death in World War I. Two generations, two wars. However, his son's tombstone features the "Stars and Stripes." (MAP: MA)

World War I Doctor, Casualty of the Spanish Flu

Dr. John Riley Lewis (August 20, 1887–September 25, 1918) practiced medicine in Gainesville for five years until he served in the Medical Reserve Corps and then was called up for active duty on January 1, 1918. His older brother, **Andy Lee** (November 27, 1886–December 25, 1936), was fighting in France at the time.

Dr. Lewis was a graduate of medical school in Fort Worth and received postgraduate work in New York and New Orleans. As an army doctor, he was a surgeon at Camp Bowie in Fort Worth. Later, he received special surgical training at Fort Riley, Kansas, and was reassigned to Fort Dix, New Jersey. There he contracted Spanish flu, which resulted in fatal pneumonia. His bride, the former **Valentine Maupin** (February 14, 1891–June 23, 1952), had accompanied him to New Jersey.

Stores closed in Gainesville for Lewis's funeral. Members of the local medical community were part of the overflow crowd of mourners. Masons and the Knights of Pythias participated in his burial. (MAP: JL)

Founder of the Tomato Clubs

Elizabeth "Lizzie" Thurman (1887–February 4, 1918), prior to the county home demonstration clubs promoted by Texas A&M, initiated "Tomato Clubs" in Cooke County to encourage girls to grow and can tomatoes. This became quite a popular program in giving farm girls an organized activity.

Lizzie was the daughter of **John W.** (July 1, 1854–February 5, 1931) and **Jennie Thurman** (July 12, 1862–November 9, 1934), who lived four miles east of Gainesville. She was active in Whaley Methodist Church. She left Gainesville in 1917 to teach in the town of Margaret in Foard County, where she died of an illness only four months after arriving. (MAP: LT)

A Tale of Two Sheriffs

Jake Wright (May 13, 1864–December 12, 1928) had just been elected to his second two-year term as sheriff when he died following a lengthy illness. He was a good friend of **Pat Ware** (Division 14) and was visited by him at his bedside at the McCain Hotel on East California Street, a short distance from the Katy Railroad tracks, where Ware was killed after his visit. Wright died a little less than two weeks after his friend was killed. (MAP: JW)

Convicted Murderer

Frank M. Bracken (November 3, 1894–February 2, 1945) shotgunned to death Gainesville fire marshal **Walter Clements** (Division 7) and motorcycle patrolman William E. Johns on July 24, 1931, in downtown Gainesville. What triggered the shooting was that Bracken was irate over being jailed earlier for a minor offense. Johns was mortally wounded, probably because he was reluctant to shoot Bracken, an old army buddy from World War I. Bracken was a charter member of the Dennis-Anderson American Legion Post when it was organized in 1920 and was its second vice-commander.

Bracken was tried and convicted for the murder of Clements in October 1931 and sentenced to ninety-nine years in prison. He obviously did not serve the complete sentence, as he died in the Gainesville sanitarium of tuberculosis in 1945. His tombstone in a family plot identifies him by his military service: "Tex. Sgt. 359 Inf. 90 Div." He was single. (MAP: FB)

Potential Hollywood Starlet

The *Los Angeles Times*'s headline read "Beauty Dies in Overturn of Machine." **Lena Mae Lane** (January 30, 1913–February 22, 1931), a potential Hollywood starlet and Houston "bathing review winner," was killed in a car wreck near Los Angeles. Lena Mae was born six miles east of Valley View, and her father worked for Tanner Furniture Company in Gainesville. When she was about twelve years old, she and her dad moved from Gainesville to Houston after the death of her mother.

In August 1930, Miss Lane represented the city of Houston in the International Bathing Pageant. Following that pageant, she and some other participants were in a personal tour that terminated in Hollywood. Lane apparently signed a movie contract with Universal Pictures shortly before her death.

Lane's companion and driver of the fatal car was twenty-six-year-old Hollywood screenwriter C. Jerome "Jerry" Horwin. He contended that the sun in his eyes caused the wreck, which resulted in the car overturning on Ventura Boulevard in Hollywood. Miss Lane was crushed to death instantly, while Horwin suffered two broken arms and severe internal injuries. Horwin was a prolific screenwriter in the 1930s and 1940s. His first movie script success was *The Pilgrim Papas* (1929). (MAP: LL)

INVENTOR OF THE "TAMALETTE"

Joanna G. Hamilton (1885–September 27, 1971), beginning about 1936, developed quite a local reputation for her chicken tamales, especially because of her success in selling cocktail tamales for a fundraiser for First Methodist Church. She was inspired while watching a movie musical called *Rio Rita*, starring two Texans, Bebe Daniels and John Boles. She decided to market her products under the name "Rio Rita Chicken Tamales and Chili." Her small, cocktail tamales were called "tamalettes" and gained a national and international reputation. One of her celebrity regulars was Guy Lombardo.

Joanna's business began in her own kitchen at 216 West Pecan Street. By 1944, she had three assistants, and they were working in a small building in her backyard, although they were planning to move her business to a "modern stucco building." (In the later 1950s, the newly organized Temple Baptist Church used the former Tamalette building as a temporary church building.) She had regular customers in the Midwest, New York, Canada and India. Her local company was purchased by the Tamalette Corporation in 1950.

This narrative is derived from Shana Powell's *Gainesville and Cooke County* and a 1944 *Register* article. (MAP: JH)

Known for His Horses and a Dog

Virgil P. Keel (1881–June 26, 1940), son of **J.Z. Keel** (Division 15), for many years was a partner with his dad in the grain business here, but Virgil's reputation was primarily associated with his success regionally as a horse trainer. He was a regular exhibitor and winner in horse shows, including Fort Worth's Southwestern Exposition and Fat Stock Show in the early 1920s. Keel's most famous horse was Kismet, which entertained thousands by jumping over an automobile. Another of his biggest award-winners was Gallant King, a five-gaited stallion.

Keel maintained a training ring at his home for the Gainesville Community Circus equestrian acts. One of Keel's "failures" as a trainer was his dog, Scotty, a Russian wolf hound. Virgil tried to train him as a jumper, but the dog flunked as a performer. Scotty sometimes would steal the show in the local circus as a dyed-pink performer that would literally lie down on the job while being led around by a clown.

Scotty gained notoriety in another way by being the subject of a district court suit in the Cooke County Courthouse. Harold Leverett sued Virgil and Mary Ellen Keel for $20,000 for being thrown out of his wagon and injured near Benjamin Franklin Elementary School. The accident, Leverett alleged, was caused by Scotty scaring his team of horses and causing them to become runaways.

The dog heard witnesses from both sides in this trial in January 1934. Conflicting witnesses testified that "he is mean and ferocious and goes around looking for trouble" and "a gentle, docile, and playful dog who loves everybody, particularly children." The *Register* described Scotty in this manner: "He would prick up his ears at times and feel he was the most important animal in town. Then at other times, he would hang his head and tuck his tail in shame." After three days of testimony, a jury decided that Scotty was not guilty. (MAP: VK)

Popular Sportswriter

William Raymond "Bill" King (May 25, 1928–December 4, 1990), a longtime sportswriter for the *Gainesville Register*, was known for his column, "King Sports." His grave marker features his signature. He was the nephew of **Morton Smith**, and his grave marker in one way imitates a feature of his uncle's tombstone in Division O. Can you figure out their similarity?

Keith King, son of Bill, continues the newspaper tradition as owner of the *Weekly News of Cooke County*. (MAP: BK)

Division 22

CSA Commander of *Niobe*

The story of **A.J. (Archibald James) Meriwether** (September 8, 1832–February 20, 1912) is remarkable. His obituary appeared in numerous newspapers, including the *St. Louis Post-Dispatch* and the *New York Times.*

Meriwether was born in Eatonton, Putnam County, Georgia, son of Judge A. and Rebecca Meriwether. He entered the United States Naval Academy at the age of fifteen.

Upon graduation, midshipman Meriwether served two years on the USS *Plymouth* in the African squadron and two years in the Mediterranean. After some United States coastal duty, he was promoted to master, the equivalent of junior lieutenant. He was stationed on the frigate *Niagara*, which brought seventy Japanese envoys to Washington in 1860. In promoting friendlier relations with Japan, Congress appropriated $50,000 for their entertainment during their seven-week visit, according to Thomas Bailey's *A Diplomatic History of the American People.*

In May 1861, Meriwether learned about Southern secession when arriving at the Boston Navy Yard. He tried to resign his commission in Washington but was refused. He rode by horseback to Richmond to report to Jefferson Davis. Assigned to the CSA *Merrimac*, he was wounded in the famous battle between the CSA *Merrimac* and the USS *Monitor*, spending three weeks in the hospital.

His next assignment involved blockade running out of Havana, Cuba. There, he received orders to sail for Marseilles, France, on the next available ship. He was ordered to the home of Confederate Colonel Livingston in Marseilles, who was married to the former Clara Gervase, whom Meriwether had rescued when she had fallen off the *Powhatan* into the Mediterranean in 1854. Meriwether jumped in after her and held her until she could be rescued. She was eternally grateful to him for saving her from a "watery grave." Now, in 1863, she, with the assistance of an uncle in the French army, insisted on giving the Confederacy a swift ship for blockade running purposes, with the provision Meriwether be made captain.

For almost two years, Meriwether commanded the French gift, the *Niobe,* on eighteen missions between Havana and various Southern ports. He lost only nine men under his command. Due to the Confederate surrender, he was under orders to scuttle the ship and its cargo out of Havana. On May 25, 1865, he put his crew into quarter boats and sank the *Niobe* at latitude sixteen degrees, ten minutes north and longitude eighty degrees, fifteen minutes west in the Caribbean. He and his crew made it to Veracruz, Mexico.

Captain Meriwether moved to Gainesville in 1868 with his wife, **Lorena Elizabeth Meriwether** (1844–1923). In his later years, Meriwether served as a police judge. He was instrumental in the movement to erect the Confederate soldier statue on the northeast corner of the courthouse square in October 1911. (MAP: AM)

The "Black Sheep's" First Victim

Tom M. Boyd (1871–April 27, 1917), a Thackerville, Oklahoma tenant farmer with six children, was fatally shot in the abdomen with a .45 pistol "during a difficulty" with **Haney Liddell** (Division 7), according to the *Register*. His death was not immediate. Boyd was brought to Gainesville from Thackerville by a convenient freight train for treatment at the Gainesville sanitarium. He died the next day. He is buried next to his sister, **Ida M. Tippitt** (1876–1967). (MAP: TB)

A School Bears His Name

Rad (Radford) A. Ware (May 1, 1861–May 27, 1925), native of Woodbine and brother of **Pat Ware** (Division 14), died after spending several weeks in Tioga in an unsuccessful attempt to seek a cure for his illness using the famous medicinal spring waters there.

Ware was a wealthy banker and large landowner whose property included a ranch in Jack County. He donated five acres of land in Woodbine for the Rad Ware Consolidated School, now the Rad Ware Elementary School, which is part of the Callisburg Independent School District.

The story has been told that the massive gray monument that marks his grave broke the wagon attempting to deliver it to the cemetery, and a piece of oil field equipment was necessary to get it to his grave site. Buried with him is his wife, **Lula Cook Ware** (January 14, 1871–July 4, 1948), a native of Missouri. Her gravestone says, "She Was a Good Woman." As a member of Whaley Methodist Church, she gave generously to a home for retired ministers in Gainesville. She was Rad Ware's fourth wife. (MAP: RW)

Division 23

People of Color

Only Black Cooke County Casualty of World War I

There is confusion about the spelling of this soldier's name. He is **John Steverson** (May 6, 1900–November 28,1918) on his grave marker. In the military records he is "Stevenson." According to the bronze plaque memorializing Cooke County casualties in the Great War on the east face of the courthouse, he is "John Steveson (colored)," and he is at the bottom of the list. That memorial plaque was added to the courthouse in 1920.

Private Steverson enlisted in the army at Fort Sill, Oklahoma, on April 8, 1918. He was stationed for a while in Virginia before being shipped overseas. He was one of the many who died of illness while serving Uncle Sam. John died of pneumonia about six months after arriving in Europe. He was in 805 Company of the 302 Stevedore Regiment. Stevedores loaded and unloaded ships. (MAP: JS)

Gravestone Representative of Mosaic Templars of America

The **Lettie Goss** (1870–January 21, 1917) grave features a well-preserved Mosaic Templars of America tombstone. The obscure insignia of the Mosaic Templars features two crossed torches with the letters "M," "T" and "A" at

This grave marker of Lettie Goss in the previously racially segregated black section represents membership in the Mosaic Templars of America. MTA was a black organization similar to Woodmen of the World.

the top. Within the lower intersection of the crossed torches is "3 Vs," which probably stands for three virtues. The bottom of the marker identifies Lettie Goss as a member of Harmony Chamber #2047, Gainesville.

There are over a dozen Mosaic Templars markers in Fairview in the previously racially segregated sections. Other local chapters mentioned on other markers are Prosperity Chamber and Star Chamber.

Mosaic Templars of America was similar to the Woodmen of the World organization, except it was an organization for blacks. John Edward Bush and Chester W. Keatts co-founded the organization in 1882 "for the purpose of elevating the colored race, socially, morally, intellectually and financially," according to A.E. Bush and P.L. Dorman's *History of the Mosaic Templars of America: Its Founders and Officials*. Its National Monument Department was founded at Tuskegee Institute in 1914. An annual fifty-cent levy financed "well designed, uniform Vermont marble" markers for its members. There was also an Endowment Department for aiding widows and orphans. By 1921, MTA was paying as much as $1,000 in death benefits to its members. Booker T. Washington helped dedicate the national headquarters in Little Rock, Arkansas. (MAP: LG)

Victim of Homicide in Front of Funeral Home

George Gamble (May 15, 1872–March 26, 1918) was gunned down by G.H. Walker, a partner in the Lindsay Hotel Barber Shop, in front of the George J. Carroll "funeral parlor" (not its current location). Gamble was sitting in his wagon and was shot four times, once in the neck, once in the abdomen and twice in the left arm. A fifth shot missed and lodged in the front door of the funeral home. Gamble's assailant fired while standing on the ground next to the wagon. Gamble attempted to get away but slid to the ground and died. He was immediately carried into the funeral home.

The *Register* on the day of the shooting reported that Walker "is a man of good character and held in high esteem by all who know him. He has made no statement, but it is said the killing resulted from the insolence of the negro to Mrs. Walker." That rumor about motivation proved to be untrue, and nothing was said about Gamble's character. Walker was released on $2,000 bond.

Walker pled not guilty to murder. He was represented by **W.O. Davis** (Division 12). The first trial scheduled for December 1918 was postponed because of the Spanish flu epidemic. A second attempt at trial was postponed because of the illness of one of the defense attorneys, John Culp.

The trial was finally held in May 1920. Approximately a dozen whites and one black testified at the trial. According to Milton Ableson, partner of Walker, there was a dispute about the amount of pay Walker was to pay Gamble for plowing a lot of his. The dispute was over whether the pay was three or five dollars and whether Gamble had done a satisfactory job. According to Ableson, Gamble got very excited while discussing the matter in their barbershop, and Walker later told his partner that he was afraid of Gamble. Ableson's wife, Ferran, also testified that she had recently seen Gamble handling a gun in a local shoe shop. The jury found Walker not guilty over two years after the offense.

Gamble's gravestone identifies him as "Mason U.B.F." (MAP: GG)

Division 24

Hebrew

One of the Founders of the Jewish Cemetery

Henry Schiff (July 5, 1836–November 7, 1930) was a longtime businessman and leader in the Gainesville Jewish community, dying at the age of ninety-four. It is interesting that the *Gainesville Register* in its initial article about his death identified him as a "pioneer" and a Mason who had been awarded a life membership by Gainesville Lodge #210 about three years before his death, but there was no mention of his religion.

Schiff was born in Hassen-Kassel, Germany, and came to America when he was about fourteen years old. He resided in New York City for about five years until he moved to Oregon to take care of the business of a deceased relative. He left Oregon after three years because his "health was none too good, owing to the damn climate."

Henry moved to St. Louis and remained there until his brother, Gus, talked him into coming to Texas. Gus was then a resident of Collin County but would eventually move to Gainesville. When Henry and Gus came to Texas, they were itinerant salesmen until Henry started a mercantile business in Dexter about 1873. When he decided Gainesville had greater potential, he moved here. He was in the dry goods business for a number of years (Schiff, Sommer & Company) and later operated a feed, grain and seed store on West California.

Henry Schiff became a leader of the newly established United Hebrew Congregation Emmanuel of Gainesville, chartered on October 25, 1881.

This fallen marker is in Division 24, the old Jewish cemetery. The lamb symbolizes innocence. Notice the Hebrew inscription.

As treasurer of that congregation, he paid the City of Gainesville $150 for one acre of land to establish a Hebrew cemetery adjacent to the city's cemetery—it didn't become part of Fairview Cemetery until June 7, 1904. The local Jewish community constructed a synagogue about 1890 on the southeast corner of North Red River Street and Broadway. An 1897 city ordinance gave the city cemetery sexton the authority to loan grave-digging tools to the sexton of the Hebrew cemetery. On March 3, 1964, the Jewish Cemetery Association gave its cemetery to the city along with $15,000 to aid in its perpetual care. (MAP: HS)

Morris Kuehn (April 1, 1844–November 1, 1881) has the earliest marked grave in the old Jewish cemetery. (MAP: MK)

"Civic Busybody"

Margaret Parx Hays (November 3, 1912–May 8, 2008) was the daughter of **Parx** and **Ianna Hays** in Division 19. In pursuing her education, Margaret did not waste time. She graduated from high school in 1929, from Gainesville Junior College in 1930 and from North Texas State Teachers College in 1931. She took advantage of the career opportunities that opened up due to World War II and began a long, distinguished career in the United States Foreign Service working in Bogota, Rio de Janeiro, Mexico City, Manila and Hong Kong.

Her retirement in 1966 led to her last career in local community service. She organized and led the Cooke County Heritage Society to save a historic

Gainesville Mayor Glenn Loch places flowers on the grave of Margaret Hays, former mayor. Both were instrumental in obtaining the Santa Fe Depot for the city and restoring it to its unique historic splendor. *With permission of Mayor Loch.*

firehouse from destruction and restore it to become the Morton Museum of Cooke County. (The museum gets its name from benefactor Granville Morton, of Morton's Potato Chip fame.) Margaret was instrumental in creating the Cooke County Mental Health Clinic in 1972 and served as its first director.

She was the first female mayor of Gainesville from 1981 to 1983. She was not part of the "good old boy system," and her habit of lecturing to those in city council meetings who didn't know the facts contributed to her being a one-term mayor.

Margaret was also a major force in the preservation of Gainesville's Santa Fe Depot. She lobbied to get Santa Fe–Burlington Northern Railroad to give its vacant depot to the City of Gainesville. With the involvement of Mayor Glenn Loch and Congressman Charles Stenholm, that happened in 1981. As president of Friends of Jones Farm from 1988 to 2000, she persistently worked for the preservation of this historic farm on the property the Johnson Branch of Ray Roberts State Park. Margaret's last project, still unfulfilled, was to build a respectfully appropriate memorial park devoted to the subject of the "Great Hanging" on the location of that event of October 1862. That location is currently in the Georgia Bass City Park on the east bank of Pecan Creek between California and Main Streets in Gainesville.

Margaret Hays, shortly before her death in 2008, was able to witness the dedication of Hays Hall, a student apartment building named in her honor on the North Central Texas College campus in Gainesville. (MAP: MH)

Division 25

People of Color

Born Slave, Died Free

There are numerous freedmen in the previously all-black, racially segregated part of Fairview Cemetery in the east section, but only one grave marker is inscribed with the slogan "Born Slave, Died Free." That is the plain, marble square that identifies the grave of **Amanda Bean** (1859–July 2, 1939). Her grave has only been identified this way since 1985, since there was no mention of this inscription in the Cross Timbers Genealogical Society book *Fairview Cemetery.* According to her death certificate, she died of senility. She lived on Commerce Street at the time of her death, and she was identified as a widow. Her death certificate identifies her occupation as "house worker." According to a Gainesville city directory, she took in laundry. This writer, in his perusing of *Gainesville Register* microfilm, knows that she also raised chickens because she reported some stolen on one occasion. (MAP: AB)

Division 26

People of Color

She Broke the Color Barrier at Gainesville Junior College

Ima Jean (Mrs. Lavan T.) Bennette (June 30, 1925–October 14, 1991), daughter of Alex and Anna Belle Becknell Johnson of Gainesville, quietly enrolled at Gainesville Junior College in 1956 and, in so doing, became the first black student at the college. She was a nontraditional student in that she was not a recent high school graduate. Mrs. Bennette had previously attended Texas College, a historic black college near Tyler, and had previously worked as a keypunch operator at Howard University in Washington, D.C. She took additional business courses here.

She was a member of St. James CME Methodist Church in Gainesville. Upon her death, her family established a college scholarship in her name. The first scholarship recipient was Kevin Mathis, who attended Texas A&M–Commerce. Later, he played defensive back in the National Football League, first for the Dallas Cowboys and later for the Atlanta Falcons and the New Orleans Saints. (MAP: IB)

Minister and Member of the Executive Board of Fort Worth NAACP

Reverend George A. Simpson Sr. (1877–August 6, 1948), former pastor of the St. James CME Church in Gainesville, preached the gospel for over thirty years. He came to Gainesville from Denton in 1906 and worked for an oil mill, the Santa Fe Depot and a grocery store before receiving the call to preach. After serving a congregation in Gainesville, he served churches in Sanger, Mount Pleasant, Wichita Falls, Sherman and Fort Worth. At the time of his death, he was president of the Interdenominational Negro Alliance in Fort Worth and was on the executive board of the National Association for the Advancement of Colored People there. (MAP: GS)

Division H

Animal Trainer, Tightrope Artist

Vern Brewer (February 28, 1912–February 21, 1993) was a multitalented animal trainer and circus performer in the Gainesville Community Circus. He trained the Liberty Horse Act, which included **Alex** and **Gerry Murrell** (Division V). Brewer was also a tightrope walker. One of his feats was jumping over a table while on the tightrope.

Brewer was a charter member of the Southwestern Shetland Pony Breeders Association. He also bred zebras and llamas, but his later specialty was miniature horses. His family has continued the miniature horse business.

As a twelve-term Gainesville city council member and ten-term mayor pro tem of the city, his pet project was the Frank Buck Zoo. (MAP: VB)

Division J

Monument Eloquent but Somewhat Misleading

The tall monument close to the front fence of Fairview that features **Lieutenant (jg) David Lamont Sims** (February 6, 1923–September 21, 1945) is eloquent but somewhat misleading. Lieutenant Sims was a decorated naval aviator who served with distinction in the Pacific during World War II. He received the Silver Star for his actions as a navy dive bomber shortly before his death and was also "credited with saving the flagship of Admiral R.K. Turner when he broke formation on a photographic reconnaissance mission to down a Japanese suicide pilot heading" toward Admiral Turner's flagship, according to the *Gainesville Register*.

It was after the formal end of World War II, however, that Lieutenant Sims was killed as a result of a collision with another navy plane over Miami. The two pilots of the F6F-3 Hellcats that collided, Lieutenant Sims of Fort Worth and Lieutenant James O'Connor of Dorchester, Massachusetts, were part of a five-plane night formation from the Melbourne, Florida naval training station. The three pilots who returned to base reported that a "mystery flight" interfered with theirs over Miami. The two downed planes crashed in the Dallas Park area of Miami a short distance from each other. One slid across a parking lot into the Tuttle garage, housing coast guard vehicles; the other crashed through the roof of the Frank T. Budge warehouse, resulting in a spectacular fire.

According to the *Orlando Star*, the planes "miraculously escaped the upper floors of hotels, some occupied by navy personnel and WAVES." Thousands of persons "lured from a wrestling match, only a few blocks away," crowded around the crash site.

David's brother, **Lieutenant Russell W. Sims Jr.**, accompanied his brother's body back to Texas. Pallbearers from the Grand Prairie Naval Air Station were participants at the funeral at First Christian Church in Gainesville.

The Sims monument declares: "In loving memory of our dear son Lt. (jg) David Lamont Sims and men of fighting squadron VC-88 who died in the wreckage of their planes far from their loved ones and the things they held dear."

Lieutenant Sims is also commemorated on the monument of World War II casualties in Leonard Park, Gainesville. (MAP: DS)

"THE JUDGE"

Carroll Fulton "Sully" Sullivant (November 24, 1902–February 23, 1978) had a distinguished career as a public servant at both the local and state levels, although he was locally known simply as "the Judge." He died of a heart attack at the age of seventy-five.

Carroll was born near Troy in Indian Territory but moved to Gainesville with his family when he was six years old. After earning his high school diploma at North Texas State Normal College (University of North Texas), he began teaching school. That was a normal course of events in the early 1900s, when schoolteachers were not required to be degreed. He taught for one year in Ivanhoe in Fannin County and two years in Hood in Cooke County. Sullivant then returned to North Texas and completed a bachelor's degree in education and English. According to the *Gainesville Register*, he worked his way through college "washing dishes and waiting on tables." His senior year, he worked part time in the library while lettering in debate.

After a brief period as a high school principal in Henrietta, he turned to law school. He distinguished himself at the prestigious Cumberland University Law School at Lebanon, Tennessee, the same law school **J.M. Lindsay** (Division 8) and **U.S. Senator Joseph Weldon Bailey** (Division

21) attended. Sullivant was president of his senior class and was supreme justice of Kappa Epsilon Phi, a legal fraternity.

Sullivant was elected to two terms in the Texas House of Representatives, serving during the 1931 and 1933 regular sessions. At the end of his second session, he resigned his seat in the legislature to become the chief administrative officer of the Texas Railroad Commission. That state agency had recently been given the power of proration to control oil production and end the chaos prevailing in the East Texas oil fields. He supervised a staff of sixteen out of an office in Kilgore. Sullivant enjoyed working under the strong leadership of Ernest O. Thompson, and when Thompson was defeated in his reelection bid in 1938, Sullivant resigned to come home to Gainesville. He brought with him his recent bride, **Adah Eloise Punchard Sullivant** (September 3, 1910–May 4, 1975), whom he married on April 28, 1938. He met Eloise while she worked in the Bureau of Vital Statistics in Austin.

From 1940 through 1948, "Sully" gained the moniker "the Judge" as judge of Cooke County and followed that with one term as county attorney. His leadership abilities were reflected in his election as president of the Cooke County Bar Association, the Texas Trial Lawyers Association and the Texas County Judges and Commissioners Association.

In 1944, the *Gainesville Register* reported the episode of Judge Sullivant coming home from work and bringing a candy bar to divide between his son Bill, who was four years old, and his sister. The candy bar was broken into two unequal pieces, and Bill took the larger of the two. The Judge admonished Bill that a gentleman would not take the bigger piece. Future attorney Bill replied, "I don't want to be a gentleman. I want to be a lawyer."

"Father knows best" also served two non-consecutive terms on the Gainesville Independent School District Board of Trustees. In 1961, Governor Price Daniel appointed him to the Board of Regents of North Texas State University (University of North Texas), where he served during the tenure of four governors until his death. In 1977, the university named its visitor center on Eagle Drive the Sullivant Visitor Center. In 2001, that building's function changed, and a new building took the Sullivant name, the Sullivant Public Safety Center at 1700 Wilshire Street, headquarters of the university's police department. (MAP: SU)

Division K

Swam the Length of the Mississippi River in 1930

Fred P. Newton (January 20, 1903–September 19, 1992) is in the *Guinness Book of World Records* for swimming the longest recorded distance in history, 1,826 miles. As a twenty-seven-year-old native of Clinton, Oklahoma, during the Great Depression, he decided to swim the length of the Mississippi River, something that had never been done. His motivation was to do something that would "make folks remember me" and possibly make some money with speaking engagements after the feat. His second goal was a failure.

The people of his hometown gave him $200 toward his financing. He anticipated the swim would take him three months to accomplish. His swimming adventure started at Ford Dam near Minneapolis on July 6, 1930, and ended in New Orleans at Carrollton Avenue on December 29, 1930. *Movietone News* captured his finish on film.

One of the factors that prolonged his swim was the fact that he had to finance his swim along the way. He frequently painted signs as a way of paying for his adventure. Much of the way, he was accompanied by his younger brother Byron in a rowboat, and he picked up another oarsman, a black man, John D. Palmer, at Cape Girardeau, Missouri. Fred's older brother, Frank, served as his advanceman for part of the way.

One of the difficulties in going down the upper Mississippi was going down a series of locks on the river. One of his biggest audiences was at the

Fred Newton is in the *Guinness Book of World Records*. In 1930, he was the first to swim the length of the Mississippi River. *Courtesy of Morton Museum of Cooke County.*

locks at Keokuk, Iowa. He also had to dodge barges along the way and was scared on one occasion by a "man-sized" gar.

During the summer he used olive oil as a skin protectant. When the water got cold, he turned to black axle grease for insulation. Wearing a black swimsuit, goggles, earplugs and coated with axle grease, this "river monster" scared quite a few kids along the bank of the river. He wore out his first swimsuit after swimming about 1,700 miles.

After the completion of his historic swim, he never attempted another marathon swim. He did work as the director of the municipal swimming pool at Clinton, Oklahoma, for several years.

Much of this account is taken from Newton's reminiscences in a *Gainesville Register* article in 1950. His wife, **Carmen**, worked for the *Register.* I personally knew Fred and did some editing of his river diary. Newton invented and patented a plastic car seat insert to take pressure off the coccyx bone. He sold this device as a Relaxo-Bak out of an office on East California Street. (MAP: FN)

Newspaperman, Circus Promoter

Joe M. Leonard (1890–December 13, 1965), son of **John T.** and **Mary Leonard** (Division 19), got in the newspaper business at the early age of five as a paper carrier. At the age of seventeen, he attended linotype school in Brooklyn, New York. His adult career with the *Gainesville Register* began in 1917.

As a four-term president of the Gainesville Chamber of Commerce, he was a persistent promoter of the Gainesville Community Circus and was active in the Texas Good Roads Association. In the spring of 1936, he accompanied Governor James Allred in a trip to the east to promote the Centennial of Texas celebration. Leonard conferred upon Vice President John Nance Garner of Texas the honor of "honorary ringmaster" of the Gainesville Community Circus. He did the same with Major Edward Bowes, host of the nationally popular *Major Bowes Amateur Hour* radio program, in New York City. Texas dignitaries, including Leonard, were in a parade in New York City hosted by Mayor Fiorello LaGuardia. (MAP: JL)

Division L

Female Oil Scout

Irene Pickler Hathaway (April 20, 1869–August 11, 1949) was born in Kirksville, Missouri. According to Shana Powell in *Gainesville and Cooke County*, Irene came to Cooke County from Kansas in 1918 as a "single, travelling encyclopedia saleslady." While here, a prospective oil man told her of the potential for oil in northeastern Cooke County. She returned to Gainesville in 1922 with representatives of Big Indian Oil Company in tow.

The former itinerant book peddler became prodigious in acquiring oil leases in the Callisburg area. After two years of unsuccessful drilling, Big Indian Oil Company threatened to give up, but Irene persuaded the company to continue for a few more months, even claiming she would personally pay the oil field workers if that were necessary. Then miraculously, on November 9, 1924, a gusher came in on Bud W. Davis's property near Callisburg. On November 11, the *Gainesville Register* editorialized: "We take off our hat to Mrs. Irene Hathaway and Captain Doudrick of the Big Indian Oil Company whenever they pass by. They stuck to their knitting, toed the mark and finally won the game hands down." That oil discovery triggered an oil boom in Cooke County, and that first oil well was active until 1970.

During her early years here, Irene lived in the Lindsay Hotel. She later bought and managed the Toy Hotel. In her later years, she resided at 510 South Morris Street with her two daughters, Mrs. Lola Blagg and **Hazel Hathaway** (1889–May 18, 1963). (MAP: IH)

Irene Hathaway established the idea that "a woman's place" was on an oil rig platform. This is Big Indian No. 2 in Callisburg, the first successful oil well in Cooke County (1924). *Courtesy of Morton Museum of Cooke County.*

DIED ON JAPANESE PRISONER OF WAR SHIP

Lieutenant Kenneth A. Bandy (1916–1944), of the Twenty-eighth Bombardment Squadron of the U.S. Army Air Corps died on a Japanese prisoner of war ship of Japan in 1944. He was a graduate of Gainesville Junior College and former student at Southern Methodist University,

He had received personal congratulations from Governor "Pappy" O'Daniel upon graduation from flight school after thirty weeks of training at Stockton Field, California, in May 1941. He was committed to three years' service, but in May 1942 he became a prisoner of war, held by the Japanese on the island of Mindinawa. About one year later, his parents were notified by the International Red Cross of his POW status. Finally, in September 1944, they were notified that he had died on a Japanese prisoner of war ship that had been bombed during the liberation of the Philippines. (MAP: BA)

None of His "Victims" Bled to Death, Barber for Fifty Years

Robert E. (R.E.) Bandy Sr. (November 30, 1885–April 30, 1967), husband of **Floy Verna Airheart Bandy** (b. October 10, 1891) and father of **Kenneth Bandy**, celebrated fifty years as a barber in 1955, although he had slowed down to working just on Thursdays and Fridays.

Prior to becoming a professional barber, he cut the hair of his family members on the family farm near Godley in Johnson County. He was good enough to trim hair for his neighbors, so he decided this was a better occupation than bailing hay during 110-degree heat, according to an interview in the *Gainesville Register.* He started as a professional barber in Godley and, after a couple of years, moved his business to Marietta, where he met his future wife. He and his family moved to Gainesville in 1914, and many of those years he did his barbering in the old Lindsay Hotel.

In 1955, Bandy recalled two particularly trying hair-cutting experiences. One involved cutting the hair of a two-year-old while on his tricycle. The other involved an unhappy customer who suggested maybe he ought to shear sheep or split rails. (MAP: BA)

Another Fratricide Plus One

Grady Carr (July 29, 1911–September 9, 1950) died a little over two weeks after being shot by his brother Benton in a domestic dispute involving Grady's wife, Polly. Benton also mortally wounded Anna Ruth Morgan, a nineteen-year-old from Fort Worth, who accompanied Grady to Benton's house at 521 Hannah, where the shooting occurred.

The *Register* account implied that Grady abused his wife. Benton reported that Polly occasionally came to his house and stayed for brief times. On the Saturday preceding the shooting, she sent some clothes to his house by taxi. She came briefly to the Benton residence on Monday morning, but Benton was unaware of that. That afternoon, Grady drove up and asked the whereabouts of his wife. Benton responded that she wasn't there. Grady returned that evening and demanded Benton bring his wife's clothes out to him. Benton said he wouldn't bring the clothes out, but he could come in and get them.

They argued about this for a while, and Grady drove off, saying he would be back. He returned shortly with Miss Morgan in the car with him. Two months earlier, Benton had filed a complaint accusing her of taking $180 from his billfold. When Anna Ruth and Grady got out of the car and approached the house, cussing, Benton came out on the front porch with his shotgun and told them to stop when they reached the front sidewalk. When they didn't stop, Benton opened fire.

Morgan, shot in the neck and face, returned to the car, attempted to get in on the driver's side and apparently fell in the street, according to one of the brothers' sisters, who witnessed the shooting. She was dead on arrival at the local sanitarium.

Grady had a slower death, suffering from forty pellet wounds to the intestines, bladder and liver. Grady ran to his car and then attempted to return to the house, falling in a muddy ditch. In his frenzy, he was "screaming for his wife and for somebody to pray for him 'because he had been a mean man.'" A grand jury "no billed" Benton on two murder charges. (MAP: GC)

GIFT OF LAND LED TO CREATION OF COUNTYWIDE COLLEGE DISTRICT

William T. Bonner (August 19, 1896–August 22, 1953) was a notable cattleman and civic leader. According to A. Morton Smith in *The First 100 Years in Cooke County*, beginning in 1927 Bonner put Cooke County on the map as a source of fine feeder stock when he shipped cattle to Iowa for feedlot fattening for the Chicago cattle market. Cattle of Cooke County origin could achieve in eighteen months a weight equivalent to what in previous years was standard for three-year-old cattle. By 1947, livestock shipped north to the Corn Belt contributed between $3 and $4 million to the Cooke County economy.

In 1927, Bonner was one of the community leaders responsible for the reestablishment of the Cooke County Fair. As a result of the Great Depression in 1933, First National Bank was reorganized as Gainesville National Bank, with Bonner as one of its directors. In Cooke County's centennial year of 1948, Bonner was actively involved in fundraising for the Sweeney Diabetic Foundation to raise money for the creation of Camp Sweeney, a diabetic camp for children east of Gainesville. Bonner personally supervised his own employees and equipment in making many improvements to the Camp Sweeney property. Those improvements included terracing, road construction and building a dam on Lake Dealey.

He was also an active leader in the Cooke County Centennial celebration, introducing Governor Coke Stevenson, who was in Gainesville to dedicate the massive ornamental entrances to Fair Park in conjunction with that event.

In 1959, he donated five acres of land west of Elm Creek to move Gainesville College from the high school campus. This led to the creation of a countywide community college district in 1960, transformed to Cooke County Junior College, Cooke County College and finally North Central Texas College.

On December 14, 1943, Bonner married **Pauline Hughes** (November 28, 1895–August 8, 1983), former superintendent of nurses at the Gainesville Sanitarium and recent superintendent of nurses at Paris Memorial Hospital. She graduated from Noyes Hospital School of Nursing in St. Joseph, Missouri, in 1920. Pauline was also a charter member of the Gainesville Soroptimist Club. (MAP: WB)

Division M

Namesake for a Lake

Hubert Hart Moss (July 5, 1892–November 27, 1952) was an educator and civic leader whose attraction to the outdoors inspired him to envision the construction of a lake to serve as a source of water for the city of Gainesville. A decade after his death, that lake that bears his name was constructed at the spot he selected at the juncture of the north and south forks of Fish Creek in northwest Cooke County.

Moss was born in Woodbine and graduated from Valley View High School. He received a bachelor of arts degree with a major in English from North Texas State Normal College and picked up another bachelor's in chemistry later. His teaching career was interrupted by World War I.

He rose in rank from a musician third class to a second lieutenant. Much of the time during his service in Europe was spent as a leader of a company of black soldiers. His chemistry students at Gainesville Junior College later appreciated his war stories in addition to teaching them chemistry. He was the consensus favorite faculty member for the first GJC graduating class in 1926.

In addition to his duties as professor of chemistry, Moss also served as treasurer of GJC from 1934 until the summer of 1946, when he was appointed Cooke County superintendent of schools. He was elected to that post in November 1946 and reelected unopposed in 1950.

On another front, he promoted the need for Gainesville to build a lake on Fish Creek, northwest of Gainesville, because Dallas claimed most of the water rights south of Gainesville. As president of the Gainesville Chamber of Commerce in 1951, he had ample opportunity to promote his lake project idea.

Construction of the Hubert H. Moss Lake began in December 1964 and was completed in September 1966. The original dam was improved after the Great Flood of 1981 threatened it. The lake's water was finally piped to Gainesville in 2001 and provides the city with 20 percent of its water needs.

Hubert Moss died as a result of a heart attack he suffered while hiking with three friends near Era on Thanksgiving Day 1952. Buried next to him is his wife and former Gainesville schoolteacher, **Annie Alderson Moss** (January 15, 1900–May 11, 1981). Their students had teased them during their days of courtship. (MAP: MO)

This essay is abridged from the application for an Official Texas Historical Marker for Hubert H. Moss on the campus of North Central Texas College.

Division MA

World War I Survivor of U-Boat Attack on SS *Tuscania*

Sidney Robert Nall (August 14, 1895–October 8, 1972), lifetime resident of Cooke County, was among the 2,156 American troops on board the troop transport SS *Tuscania* when it was sunk off the northern coast of Ireland by German *UB-77* on the evening of February 5, 1918.

The SS *Tuscania* was originally a passenger liner of over 1,400 tons built for the Cunard Steamship Line in 1914. Its last voyage as a camouflaged troop transport originated in Hoboken, New Jersey, carrying troops from Camp Merritt, Dumont, New Jersey. Its destination was Liverpool. In addition to the 2,100 American troops, it carried thirty mules, supply wagons, bacon, airplane parts and a crew of over 200.

UB-77, with a crew of 37, was able to penetrate a British-American convoy of twenty-two vessels and get off one successful torpedo hit. The *Tuscania*'s loss of only 210 was largely due to its watertight compartments' ability to keep it afloat long enough for most to abandon ship and due to the prompt action of convoy ships in rescuing survivors.

The *Gainesville Register* briefly reported Nall as "missing in action." After the war, Nall had a career as a carpenter in Cooke County. He died in the Veterans Hospital in Dallas over fifty years after his brush with death at sea. (MAP: SN)

Division N

KILLED DURING WORLD WAR II TRAINING

Corporal Robert R. Livingston (April 6, 1924–August 9, 1943) was fatally injured in an explosion while he was setting dynamite charges during army training at Camp Leonard Wood, Missouri. He was a member of the 291 Anti-Tank Battalion of the Seventy-fifth Division. Ironically, on the day of his fatal injury, Corporal Livingston received notification that he had been accepted for Officer Candidate School.

As a Gainesville youth, he was a paper boy for the *Gainesville Register.* After graduation from Gainesville High School, he worked doing construction at Camp Howze before entering the military service. His parents were summoned and arrived at the soldier's bedside prior to his demise. Robert's father, **Robert C.** (September 28, 1896–December 19, 1981), was vice-commander of the Dennis-Anderson American Legion Post in Gainesville. (MAP: RL)

Division O

–30–

Alex Morton Smith (November 7, 1903–April 7, 1957) was a longtime editor of the *Gainesville Daily Register*, author of *The First 100 Years of Cooke County* and a founder of the Gainesville Community Circus. Appropriately, the "—30—" inscription on his tombstone is a mark of the journalistic profession, meaning "end of the story."

Morton Smith was the son of Alex Montague Smith, a traveling shoe salesman from Marysville, and Stella Green Smith. He was a great-great-grandson of Daniel Montague, pioneer surveyor, foreman of the "Great Hanging" jury and namesake of Montague County.

Smith began his career at the *Gainesville Register* shortly after high school graduation and worked his way up to city editor two years later and managing editor in 1942. His hallmark was his daily newspaper column, "Town Topics," which highlighted local happenings.

Cooke County officially celebrated its centennial on March 20, 1948. Smith, as chairman of that centennial celebration, was inspired to compile his *First 100 Years of Cooke County*. The nucleus of that book was based on the fiftieth anniversary–edition of the *Gainesville Register* published on September 23, 1940, and the massive Cooke County Centennial Edition of the *Register* published on August 30, 1948, which mentioned over fifteen thousand persons deceased and living. Morton fought the effects of a stroke he suffered in 1951 to finish his book and work at the *Register* until five months before his death.

At his death, the Smith family received a multitude of telegrams and letters of condolence from both the circus world and the journalism world. Among them was one from Warren K. Agee, chairman of the Journalism Department of Texas Christian University, who was appreciative of the "sage advice and kindly encouragement" Morton gave to his students during their annual visit to the offices of the *Register.* **Bill King** (Division 21), nephew of Morton, in his *Register* sports column, "King Sports," declared: "When the whistle sounds for the Big Show up there, we know the Great Ringmaster will lead Morton to a seat of honor."

Smith's involvement in Gainesville's Little Theatre, both as a director and actor, resulted in Morton Smith's marriage to **Mary Louise Shriver Smith** (February 16, 1902–September 25, 1963) and the founding of the Gainesville Community Circus. Inspired by a discontinued Chautauqua series, John S. Hardy, Morton Smith and others formed the Little Theatre to provide live dramatic entertainment to area residents in the spring of 1924. Louise Shriver, native of Nashville, Tennessee, came to Gainesville in 1925 and in a short time became a popular actress in the Little Theatre, especially popular with Morton Smith. Their wedding on December 8, 1926, was the "talk of the town."

The Little Theatre flourished until about 1930, when sound motion pictures pushed the theatrical group off the stage of the Majestic Theater. Morton, who was a circus enthusiast from the time he was a boy and played circus with toy animals, came up with the idea of the theatrical group performing an indoor circus parody as a fundraiser possibly to build a facility for the group. Their performances as a circus were so popular that the circus took the place of the theatre organization. Morton became the circus ringmaster, and Louise became the first female clown in the circus. The Gainesville Community Circus toured regionally as an amateur circus for over two decades and received national publicity. Its demise was due largely to a fire in 1954 that destroyed much of its equipment.

The Smiths acquired a large collection of circus memorabilia due to their circus experiences. The Circus Fans of America held its annual convention in Gainesville in 1952 and elected Morton Smith its president.

Louise was a companion to her husband in his major endeavors. Morton was active as a member of Whaley United Methodist Church from his teenage years, serving in various capacities, including ushering at the south door of the church for twenty-five years. Louise also served the church in various capacities, including Sunday school teacher. She also worked on the staff on the *Gainesville Register* for three years after Morton's death. She was a civic leader in her own right. She served as president of the Business and Professional Women's Club and was active in Friends of the Library and the Cooke County chapter of the American Cancer Society.

The Smiths were survived by two sons: Daniel Montague Smith and Jerry Green Smith. (MAP: MS)

Division S

Died with the Five Sullivan Brothers on the USS *Juneau* during World War II

George Warren Parten (January 12, 1922–November 13, 1942), pharmacist's mate, third class, is honored with a gravestone adjacent to that of his parents, **Charles W.** (February 7, 1889–March 22, 1947) and **Mary E.** (b. December 20, 1896). George's stone was erected shortly after the death of his father.

George was assigned to the light cruiser USS *Juneau* (CL-52) along with five Sullivan brothers from Waterloo, Iowa, who insisted on serving on the same ship, in violation of the usual navy policy that prohibited that. The *Juneau* was a participant in the battle over Guadalcanal in the Pacific. The *Juneau* survived one Japanese torpedo hit near the forward fire room. Severely disabled, it attempted to struggle away from the battle with water at its bowline. On the following day, a torpedo aimed at the USS *San Francisco* missed it and struck the *Juneau* near its previous torpedo hit. The *Juneau* was blown in half, killing most of the crew.

About 115 men survived the ship's sinking, but the other American ships left the area for fear of concentrated Japanese attacks. There was much controversy when the details of what happened were learned by the public. Help finally came to the men left in the sea a shocking eight days after the sinking of the *Juneau.* There were only ten survivors who managed to live despite exposure, exhaustion and shark attacks. It is unclear whether Parten was killed on board or died later at sea. (MAP: GP)

This monument marks a cenotaph, an empty grave, for George Parten. He was on the USS *Juneau*, sunk by the Japanese during World War II. Only ten of the crew survived.

Killed Aboard USS *Saint Paul* during the Korean War

Bobby Joe Cole (April 30, 1932–April 21, 1952), seaman in the United States Navy, was among thirty sailors killed in a fire in forward gun turret #8 on the USS *Saint Paul* during a fire support operation near the port of Wonson, North Korea. Most of the sailors died of asphyxiation.

Cole was a little more than one week shy of his twentieth birthday. He was killed one year to the day of the beginning of his service in the navy. Cole attended Gainesville High School. His father, J.B. Cole, formerly the proprietor of a café on North Commerce Street in Gainesville, was engaged in farming east of Gainesville at the time.

The USS *Saint Paul*, "the Fighting Saint," had the honor of firing the last naval volley of the Korean War, one minute before the truce was signed on July 27, 1953. (MAP: BC)

Division V

Why G.S. Beaver Went by His Initials

If you were born in Georgia in 1865 and your parents named you **General Sherman**, when you came of age you would probably go by **G.S. Beaver** (October 5, 1865–August 4, 1948), too. Why would native Georgians name a son for a Yankee general who devastated much of Georgia in 1864? The family has been puzzled by it; however, it makes sense knowing that G.S.'s father, Thomas, was wounded in fighting for the Confederacy and went home to recuperate. He was listed as "absent without leave" for the December 11, 1863 roll call. His wife, Frances, hid him out in a hollow log for six weeks to prevent him from having to return before he had recuperated, according to family history. It is not clear whether he ever returned to his military unit. Perhaps, he was grateful for General Sherman's efforts to bring the war to a swift conclusion, hence the son, "General Sherman."

G.S.'s family moved to Arkansas sometime after 1872, where he grew to adulthood and married Anne Seebole. They moved to the Waco-Brenham area, where he had various jobs: operating a streetcar, working in a furniture factory and helping maintain county roads. G.S. and Anne had six children, three of them dying of measles in infancy. Anne died shortly after the death of her third child, who also died in infancy.

In 1900, G.S. married **Frieda Tiede Kretzschmar** (1872–1974). He brought three children to the marriage; she brought one. Shortly after their marriage, they moved to the Marysville-Bulcher area in northwest Cooke

County. They farmed, growing cotton, corn, grain and a family garden. This marriage produced eight children, with one son named simply "Sherman." They finally settled in the Rock Creek community on the Walnut Bend Road in northeastern Cooke County, continuing farming.

In 1941, G.S. bought a plot in Fairview and constructed a concrete grave marker with a date of "10, 18, 41" on it. Cemetery observers were puzzled by the inscription until he explained it to the *Gainesville Register*. That date was supposed to represent the date he erected the marker, although he got the date wrong. He "expressed the belief that dates of birth and death on grave stones were unnecessary." G.S. died of cancer seven years later. The family later replaced the handcrafted stone with a large commercial stone. Frieda lived to be 102 years old, dying in 1974. (MAP: GS)

Much of this narrative is from an unpublished Beaver family history written by David Clifton and grandson Randel Beaver of Archer City, Texas.

"Murdered" on His Tombstone

The story of **James Russell Washington Jr.** (August 8, 1870–January 8, 1892) and his brother John is another example of a "Cain and Abel" situation. John shot and killed his brother James in the Dexter area over a dispute about a fence. Jake Brazelton, a witness, escaped being killed because John's gun was empty. John Washington was never located by the authorities. The first rumor was that he was hiding out in Indian Territory. According to his family, he lived in obscurity in New Mexico Territory. (MAP: JW)

Girl on the White Horse

Geraldine "Gerry" Finnie Murrell (July 26, 1902–August 21, 1950) is buried with her parents, **Carrie Lou** (1875–January 27, 1945) and **E. Gip Finnie** (1876–August 22, 1955), and her husband, **Alex Murrell** (1902–July 21, 1964). Gerry was born on the birthplace of her father at Spring Creek, south of Gainesville. She graduated from Gainesville High School and married Alex Murrell on October 1, 1923. They made their home at the Murrell family residence at 1202 South Lindsay.

A featured equestrian act of the Gainesville Community Circus included, *left to right*, Vern Brewer (Division H) and Gerry and Alex Murrell. *Courtesy of Morton Museum of Cooke County.*

Gerry was one of the five founders of the Gainesville Community Circus. During World War II, she worked during the day at the Camp Howze post office and at night as a nurse's aide in the Camp Howze hospital. She taught Sunday school at First Methodist Church for over twenty years.

Her affinity with animals, especially horses, dated back to her upbringing on the farm. She was a member of the Hobby Horse Club and a contributor to the *Shetland Pony Journal*, but her claim to fame was as "the girl on the white horse (Sun D.)" in the Gainesville Community Circus. They performed at rodeos, horse shows and parades in addition to the circus. In 1946, they performed in the Fireman's Circus in the Rose Bowl. "The Blue Danube Waltz," her favorite piece of music for equestrian performances, was played at her funeral.

She died from a lengthy illness. Her co-workers at Texas Power and Light Company; Morton Smith, circus colleague; and C.H. Leonard, publisher of the *Gainesville Register* where Gerry worked in the advertizing department, served as pallbearers. As a posthumous honor, a young elephant acquired by the Frank Buck Zoo was named "Gerry" in her honor. "Girl on the White Horse" appears on her grave marker.

Alex, son of **Jesse** and **Ada Murrell** (Division 4), was part of Gerry's equestrian act. He was also the circus equipment manager. Much of that equipment was homemade. He was superintendent for Texas Power and Light for many years. His grave marker bears the Masonic emblem. (MAP: MU)

"Man Without a Country"

For almost seventy years, **Paul Hugon** (October 12, 1863–September 4, 1950) was a person without a country. He was born in Montevideo, Uruguay, at a time when it had no recognized government. His parents had fled to South America because of the French government's persecution of French Huguenots. He came to America with his parents, settling at first in Missouri when he was eleven years old. They moved to Texas in 1878 and settled in Cooke County in 1880.

He began voting in Texas in 1888, after filing a Declaration of Intention to become a United States citizen, and continued voting despite complications in the process of becoming a citizen. The *Gainesville Register* on December 3, 1942, reported that Hugon would become a citizen before the end of the year.

Paul Hugon died in 1950 and was survived by son David, a resident of Venezuela; son Felix of Denison; daughter Mrs. Ruth Nichols of Waco; and daughter Esther Findley of Gainesville. Gwendolyn (Mrs. Ralph) Sidener of Gainesville is his granddaughter. (MAP: PH)

Prominent Merchant Killed in Car-Tractor Wreck

Arthur Teague Sr. (September 8, 1875–May 25, 1942), longtime pioneer merchant in Gainesville, died of a brain concussion suffered in a car-tractor wreck involving a car driven by his son, Phillip, and a farm tractor driven by James Davis Aughtry on U.S. Highway 77 two miles north of Sanger. Mr. Aughtry of the Lois community also died. The wreck occurred when the Teague vehicle attempted to pass the tractor and Aughtry attempted to cross the road in front of the car.

Teague's career in business is another example of the Horatio Alger kind of story. About 1895, he came from Lexington, Tennessee, via St. Louis to Gainesville. When he left home, his immediate goal was to be a drummer (traveling salesman). He had a bad experience in St. Louis, went to the train station there and, on a hunch, bought a Katy ticket to Gainesville.

Shortly after arriving here broke, he introduced himself to **George Y. Bird** (Division 4) at Bird's General Store. It so happened that Teague's father had loaned Mr. Bird a mule and buggy for a day when Bird was on business in Tennessee. Arthur reminded Bird of that. Bird gave him a job clerking in his store. Teague earned ten dollars a month and was able to save three or four dollars a month from his pay.

Teague was a hard worker and ambitious. After working a while in Bird's store, he tried his hand as a traveling shoe salesman for one year. He didn't like that kind of work, so he returned to retail sales working for R.J.M. Patterson's department store and later for **Val Peers** (Division 20). On July 22, 1903, he married **Anna Francis Hines** (1876–May 11, 1960), who was a clerk in a competitor's store.

On February 2, 1912, Arthur Teague opened the Teague Company store. At the time of his death, it was the longest continuously operating department store in Gainesville. Teague liked to brag that it was the first "one price department store in Gainesville." He told employees that everyone paid the same price, even his mother. A refurbished Teague Company sign can still be seen on the Elm Street side of Gainesville Title Company at 115 North Dixon. (MAP: AT)

Gainesville School Superintendent and Early College President

Hugh O. McCain Sr. (August 26, 1878–July 21, 1954), Gainesville High School principal, became Gainesville school superintendent and Gainesville Junior College president under strained circumstances at the end of the 1927–28 school year. He was replacing Lee Clark, who left because of a cut in salary. Eleven faculty members also quit. McCain mastered the situation and served as superintendent and college president for over a decade and a half.

The junior college emphasized economical education, and the college survived some rough years under McCain's guidance. For some people, the

Depression started before the stock market crash of 1929. McCain fully realized the value of the local college. Five of his children (Ida, Eula, Hugh Jr., Clyde and Mary) attended the college.

McCain, as president of the college during World War II, had to cope with numerous unusual circumstances. In response to war demands, the college created an aeronautics program. All of the first graduates of that program passed the test to receive their pilots' licenses. In late September 1942, McCain let out all schools, including the college, for most of one week so that faculty, staff and students could go to the fields and pick cotton. There was a severe labor shortage and a fear that the cotton wouldn't get picked. Pay for picking cotton was $1.50 per 100 pounds; pay for pulling bolls was $1.00 per 100 pounds. The 1944 college graduation class consisted of eight women. Many of the male students or potential students had entered the military. (MAP: HM)

Division W

Namesake of Garden Club

Margaret R. "Maggie" House (July 8, 1889–July 3, 1979) is probably better remembered than her husband because of her efforts to beautify Gainesville. From a backyard meeting she had on South Grand with **Anna May Wherry** (Division U), they created the first women's garden club in Gainesville. They founded the club on April 28, 1931, and in 1934 it became affiliated with the State Federation of Garden Clubs. The club took the name Maggie House Garden Club, and Anna May Wherry became the club's first chairwoman.

In a November meeting in 1935, Maggie appealed to the public to contribute approximately $1,000 for beautifying an addition to Leonard Park to extend to Fair Park. Recent WPA funds of $11,000 would pay for curbing and driveways, but no flowers. Numerous club members had already contributed crape myrtles and red bud trees. The club was also requesting donations of iris, cannas and dwarf plume grass. Maggie suggested that the clubs of Gainesville beautify other parts of Gainesville under the club's advisement.

The club is still active today. In years past, it has sponsored annual garden shows, held educational meetings monthly and toured homes and public gardens to enlighten members.

Maggie's husband, **Louis Albert House** (May 23, 1883–February 24, 1944), was a Gainesville cotton buyer who became Gainesville's first city manager in 1928 and served until 1936. (MAP: HO)

PIONEER FUNERAL HOME DIRECTOR

When **George J. Carroll** (1878–December 2, 1952) died, he had been in the mortuary business in Gainesville for a little over a half century. Born in Dallas, his father, T.W. Carroll, operated a gristmill north of Dallas. The site of his father's mill became Carrollton, named for his father.

George was one of the first licensed embalmers in Texas and Oklahoma, receiving his training in Chicago in 1901, according to Joe M. Leonard Sr. in the *Register.* At the time of his death, Carroll was a member of the Texas Funeral Directors Association, the National Funeral Directors Association and the National Selected Morticians. George J. Carroll and Son Funeral Home, although not the only funeral home in Gainesville, had the first funeral home specifically built for that purpose. The company is a responsible repository of thousands of burial records.

An early twentieth-century itemized statement form from his funeral home reveals changes in mortuary practices over the years. It includes the

George J. Carroll, standing in front of his funeral home's ambulance/hearse, circa 1930. In those days, funeral homes transported both the living and the dead. *Courtesy of George J. Carroll & Son Funeral Home.*

following options: burial robe, burial slippers and hose, washing and dressing, shaving, keeping body on ice, disinfecting rooms, carriage or automobile transportation to the cemetery, candelabrum and candles. George Carroll also invented and manufactured a grave cover to cover the bare earth around a grave with a fabric resembling artificial grass. He manufactured this device in 1927 after having used it for over two years. According to the *Register*, it featured "a special fibre found in France and later specially treated in German chemical plants to waterproof it and give it the color and appearance of greenest grass." According to Scott Flanagan, Carroll also invented a device to lower the casket into the grave.

Carroll was active in his city in numerous ways in addition to providing funeral services for the bereaved. According to Leonard, he organized, coached and played on the first football team in Gainesville. "It was composed of Gainesville young men and brought prominence to the city by reason of the many games it won against outside competition. Regulation football garb was scarce in those days and some of the members of the local group played barefoot or in socks." According to Morton Smith, they practiced on gravel streets on the southeast corner of the courthouse square and played their games at Kanetso Park.

Carroll was also a promoter of the Gainesville Boys Band, which numbered 150 members in the early 1920s. It claimed to be the "world's largest boy band" and appeared on radio and performed at Mineral Wells, Galveston and the Fort Worth Fat Stock Show. He was also one of the organizers of the Gainesville Community Circus and was its first president, according to Morton Smith. And he was a charter member of the Gainesville Rotary Club, a Mason, a member of the Hella Shrine Temple in Dallas and a "longtime member of the Leeper Lake Club in Southern Oklahoma," according to Leonard.

George J. Carroll was a quietly generous man who helped people who couldn't afford funerals and also helped young people continue their education. Shortly after entering the funeral profession in Gainesville, he married **Rosa B. Ware** (d. January 12, 1962) in 1903. She was the daughter of **Pat** and **Matilda Ware** (Division 14). (MAP: GC)

REPORTEDLY, FIRST TEXAS AGGIE KILLED IN WORLD WAR II

First Lieutenant Dennis "Dennie" Hawkins Woodruff (November 11, 1916–April 24, 1942), son of A.C. and **Leola B. Woodruff**, was killed instantly at 4:55 a.m. on April 24, 1942, when his plane collided with another on the ground at Fort Richardson, Alaska. Visibility was extremely poor, and the control tower gave Woodruff permission to take off, even though the control tower could not see the planes on the ground.

According to local Aggie Van Knight, Woodruff was the first Texas Aggie killed in World War II. In addition to being an Aggie, he was a graduate of

Lieutenant Dennis Woodruff is reportedly the first Texas Aggie to be killed in World War II. His plane collided with another plane on the ground under foggy conditions in Alaska. *Courtesy of his brother, Don Woodruff.*

Gainesville Junior College, class of 1936. Lieutenant Woodruff trained as a pilot at Tulsa and Kelly Field in San Antonio. He received his wings at Randolph Field, also at San Antonio. He had been in the service for two years and married the former Dorothy Jane Newton while he was stationed at Hamilton Field, California. She last visited him in Alaska in March 1942.

On Monday, April 27, 1942, at 7:00 p.m., a memorial service was conducted at First Methodist Church by Reverend W. Harrison Baker, former pastor, simultaneously with a funeral service at Anchorage, Alaska, held at 2:00 p. m. their time. In salute to their fallen comrade, five U.S. Army Air Corps planes from Perrin Field in Sherman flew over the church. One of them was piloted by W. Harrison Baker Jr.

Lieutenant Woodruff was privately reburied in Fairview on September 29, 1948, when other World War II casualties were coming home to their final resting place. (MAP: DW)

Division XA

First Elected Female County Official

Alice Josephine (Culberson) Thomason (June 2, 1890–December 2, 1962) was born in Indian Territory. She married **W. Monroe Thomason** (May 18, 1888–December 21, 1971) on October 15, 1911. Alice was the first woman elected county official in Cooke County, elected to two terms as county treasurer in 1926 and 1928. (MAP: TH)

Unknown Grave Locations

Unsuccessful in Saving Boy from Cave-in

John Ray (d. December 5, 1918), a local well digger, and John Penrod, a Thackerville boy, died from a cave-in when they were digging an underground silo on the farm of John Mahan, a Gainesville lumberman, "about one mile north of the new Red River bridge" in Oklahoma. The two bodies were recovered in twenty feet of sand beneath the surface, according to the *Gainesville Register.* Workers labored for about five hours to recover the bodies, having to brace the walls where they were digging to prevent another cave-in.

John Ray was found in a kneeling position, attempting to shield the boy from the cave-in. One upraised arm attempted to shield the boy, while his other arm wrapped around the head of the boy. John Ray was survived by his wife and one child. George J. Carroll & Son Funeral Home records indicate that Ray is buried in Fairview, but he is missing from the cemetery records. Mahan paid Ray's funeral cost, $107. The boy, John Penrod, is buried in a cemetery west of Thackerville.

Baby Thrown by Mother from a Train

Joyce Elizabeth Carlton (December 14, 1919–February 13, 1920) was a two-month-old infant who was thrown by her despondent, nineteen-year-old mother, Sarah Bell Carlton, from a westbound Katy passenger train, three miles east of Gainesville. A Katy section crew member, "Joe Felton, colored," discovered the baby girl by the railroad tracks shortly after she was tossed, and Katy employee S.G. Staniforth brought the baby to the sheriff's office, where she was examined by **Dr. C.B. Thayer** (Division L). Baby Carlton died several hours later in the Gainesville sanitarium. George J. Carroll Funeral Home and Miss Carlton's relatives took care of the burial. Mr. and Mrs. W.H. Ellison of Muenster were Sarah Carlton's stepfather and mother.

A Katy brakeman testified that the young woman got on the train with a baby in Denison and exited the train in Muenster without the baby. After an interrogation of the mother by County Attorney Jones and Marshal Loving in Muenster, she was brought back to Gainesville and locked up in the county jail, with bail being set at $2,000. Justice of the Peace **J.P. Hall** (Division 14) conducted an inquest and ruled cause of death due to being thrown from the train, based on her mother's confession.

Miss Carlton was a remorseful, unwed mother, and when the facts of the case came out, according to the *Register*, there was much local sympathy about her plight "for the unfortunate girl…who has been sinned against more than she has sinned herself." "Twelve prominent business men" took care of her bail to obtain her release.

Sarah, who was on her way home to Muenster from Louisville, Kentucky, birthplace of her infant, confessed that she entered the ladies' restroom on the train about three miles from Gainesville and threw her baby out the window. Her trial was held on May 20, 1920, in the Cooke County Courthouse. The county attorney reduced the murder charge to manslaughter. Manslaughter was defined as homicide under "immediate influence of sudden passion arising from adequate cause." Sarah pled guilty and was sentenced from two to five years in the state penitentiary.

E
N
S
W
D
P
R
XA
AT
X
E
O
MS
S
BC
GP
8
TB
WP
JD
AWBA
JJ
CB
F
NA
N
RL
G
MA
SN
MO
M
T
7
BI
HL
JE
LO
WL
MT
KH
WC
HU
6
6A
U
H
VB
K
FN
JL
WB
GC
L
BA
IH
V
GS
HM
AT
PH
GI
JW
MU
GC
HO
DW
W
J
DS
SU

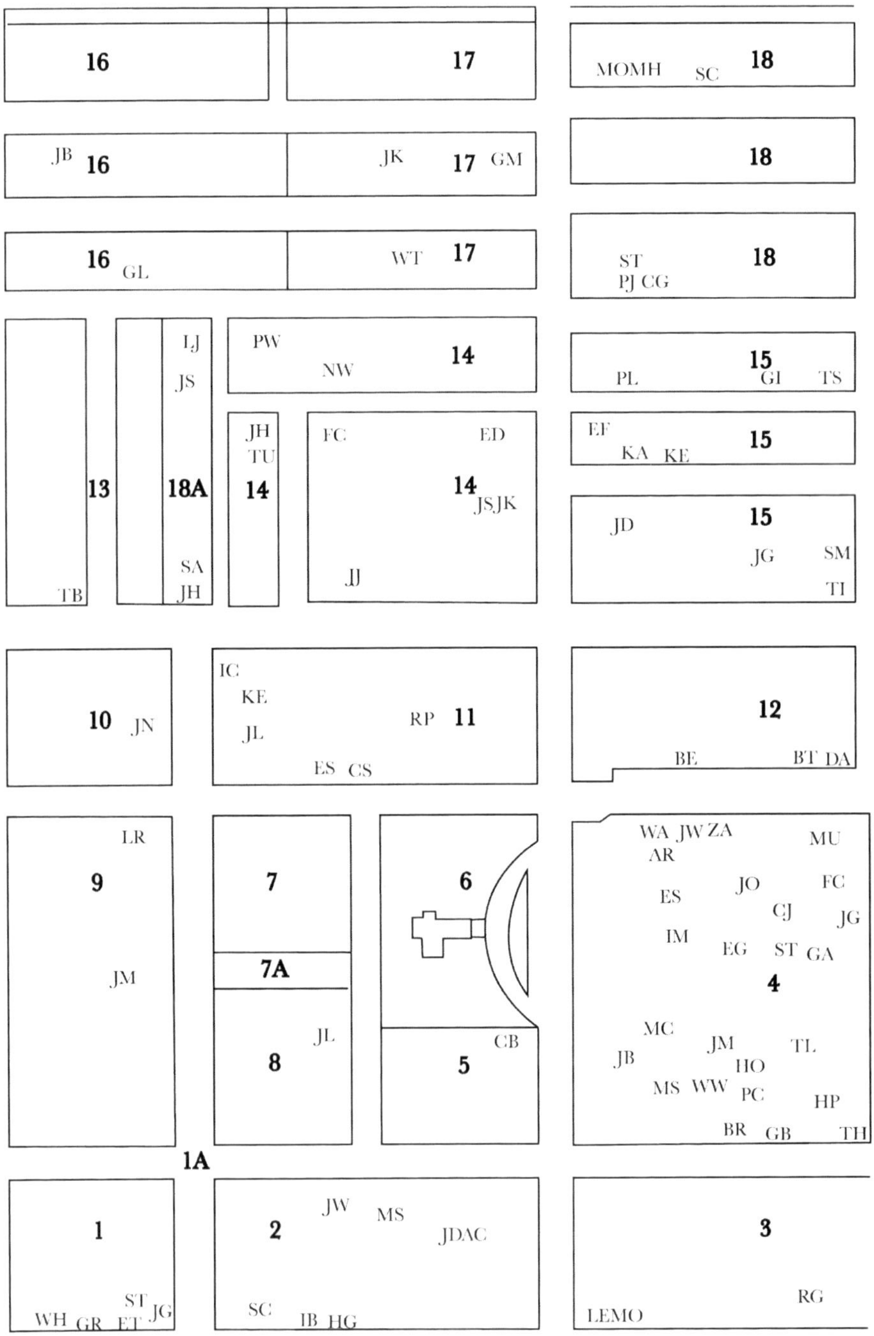
16
17
MOMH
SC
18
JB
16
JK
17
GM
18
16
GL
WT
17
ST
PJ CG
18
LJ
JS
PW
NW
14
15
PL
GI
TS
JH
TU
FC
ED
EF
KA
KE
15
13
18A
14
14
JS JK
15
JD
JG
SM
TB
SA
JH
JJ
TI
IC
KE
10
JN
JL
RP
11
12
ES
CS
BE
BT
DA
LR
WA
JW
ZA
MU
AR
9
7
6
JO
FC
ES
CJ
JG
IM
EG
ST
GA
JM
7A
4
MC
JL
CB
JM
TL
JB
8
5
HO
MS
WW
PC
HP
BR
GB
TH
1A
JW
MS
1
2
JDAC
3
RG
ST
JG
WH
GR
ET
SC
IB
HG
LEMO

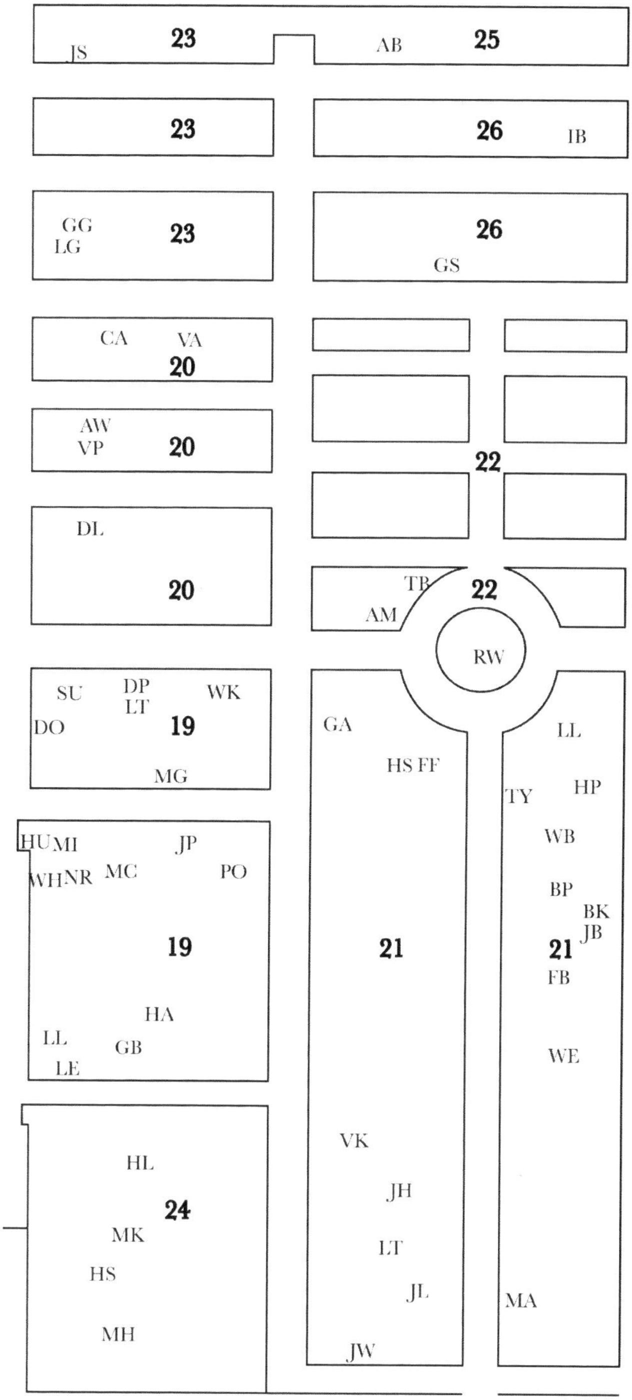

JS
23
AB
25
23
26
IB
GG
LG
23
26
GS
CA
VA
20
AW
VP
20
22
DL
20
TB
22
AM
RW
SU
DP
LT
WK
DO
19
MG
GA
HS FF
LL
TY
HP
HU
MI
JP
WH
NR
MC
PO
WB
BP
BK
JB
19
21
21
FB
HA
LL
GB
LE
WE
HL
24
MK
HS
MH
VK
JH
LT
JL
JW
MA

Addington, W.H.H.	Division 4, WA
Addington, Zach	Division 4, ZA
Austin, Belle	Division 8 (East of 7), BA
Bailey, Joseph Weldon & Ellen	Division 21, JB
Bandy, Kenneth	Division L, BA
Bandy, R.E., Sr.	Division L, BA
Bean, Amanda	Division 25, AB
Beaver, G.S.	Division V, GS
Beckelman, Jacob	Division 4, JB
Belcher, Harry & Sallie	Division 12, BE
Bennette, Ima Jean	Division 26, IB
Bier, Augusta & Henry	Division 7, BI
Bird, George Y. & Elizabeth	Division 4, GB
Bischoff, George & Mollie	Division 19, GB
Blanton, W.L. & Gertrude	Division 21, WB
Bonner, William T. & Pauline	Division L, WB
Bosley, Clifford	Division 8 (East of 7), CB
Boyd, Tom M.	Division 22, TB
Bracken, Frank	Division 21, FB
Braswell, John Charles	Division 16, JB
Brewer, Vern	Division H, VB
Brook, Tommy	Division 8 (East of 7), TB
Brown, Tom	Division 13, TB (unmarked)
Bunch, infant of E.F.	Division 2, IB (unmarked)
Burch, Cecil	Division 5, CB
Carlton, Joyce Elizabeth	unknown grave location
Carr, Grady	Division L, GC
Carrington, Andrew	Division 2, AC
Carroll, George J. & Rosa	Division W, GC
Cassady, Emma & Hopkins	Division 20, CA
Chevalier, infant of	Division 11, IC
Cleaves, Frank & Dallas	Division 4, FC
Clements, J. Walter	Division 7, WC
Cole, Bobby Joe	Division S, BC
Collard, F.E.	Division 14, FC (unmarked)
Conlee, Martha	Division 19, MC
Conlee, Preston	unknown grave location
Cox, Mary Josephine	Division 4, MC
Crooks, Thomas J.	Division 19, PO

Darwin, Elizabeth Lee	Division 14, ED
Davenport, James B., Jr.	Division 15, JD
Davis, Joseph P., Jr.	Division 8 (East of 7), JD
Davis, W.O. & family	Division 12, DA
Dougherty, F.M. & family	Division 19, DO
Dougherty, Isaac Newsome	Division 19, DO
Dougherty, William H.	Division 19, DO
Drake, James W.	Division 2, JD
Emerson, William	Division 21, WE
Estes, John M.	Division 7, JE
Finch, Ed	Division 15, EF
Fleenor, "Fatty" & family	Division 21, FF
Gallia, Tincie family	Division 4, GA
Gamble, George	Division 23, GG
Garmany, W.H.	Division 21, GA
Garrett, John & family	Division 15, JG
Gerard, Ernest	Division 4, EG
Gerard, Joseph	Division 4, JG
Gibson, Homer	Division 2, HG (unmarked)
Gilbert, Rachel Gibbs	Division 3, RG
Gilcreest, Jacob Edward & family	Division 15, GI
Goss, Lettie	Division 23, LG
Greenwood, Catherine	Division 18, CG (unmarked)
Grimes, John	Division 1, JG (unmarked)
Hall, J.P. & family	Division 14, JH
Hall, Kenneth	Division 7, KH (unmarked)
Hamilton, Joanna	Division 21, JH
Hathaway, Irene	Division L, IH
Hays, Margaret Parx	Division 24, MH
Hays, Parx & Ianna	Division 19, HA
Hickman, Tom & family	Division 4, TH
Hickson, J.L.	Division 18A, JH
Hill, Lula	Division 18, MO
House, Maggie & Louis	Division W, HO
Houston, Mary	Division 18, MH
Howeth, William & family	Division 4, HO
Hudson, William	Division 19, WH
Hughes, C.T. & family	Division 19, HU
Hughes, Roy	Division 19, HU

Hugon, Paul	Division V, PH
Hulen, Gene & Harvey	Division 6, HU
Jirasek, James	Division 8 (East of 7), JJ
Jirasek, Leon	Division 18A, LJ
Johnson, C.J.	Division 4, JO
Johnson, Powell	Division 18, PJ (unmarked)
Jones, C.N. & Sara	Division 4, CJ
Kaden, Herman & family	Division 15, KA
Kaden, James	Division 14, JK
Kammerdiener, Johnnie Ruth	Division 17, JK
Keel, J.Z.	Division 15, KE
Keel, Virgil	Division 21, VK
Kennedy family	Division 11, KE
King, William Raymond "Bill"	Division 21, BK
Kinne, William B.	Division 19, WK
Kuehn, Morris	Division 24, MK
Lacy, D.T.	Division 20, DL
Lane, Grace	Division 16, GL (unmarked)
Lane, Lena Mae	Division 21, LL
Lee, Lawrence & Mary	Division 19, LL
Leeper, J.D.	Division 19, LE
Leeper, Nettie	Division 19, LE
Lefkowitz, Hirshell	Division 24, HL
Leonard, Joe M., Sr.	Division K, JL
Lewis, John Riley	Division 21, JL
Liddell, Haney & family	Division 7, HL
Light, J.Y.	Division 11, JL
Lindsay, J.M.	Division 8, JL
Lindsay, Tennie Bonner	Division 4, TL
Livingston, Robert R.	Division N, RL
Locke, W. Herbert	Division 7, WL
Long, J. Pope	Division 15, PL
Looney, Mary Ann	Division 15, GI
Mahan, Jack	Division 9, JM
Manahan, James Arthur	Division 21, MA
Manahan, J.R. & Anna	Division 21, MA
McAdams, Sam	Division 15, SM
McCain, Hugh O.	Division V, HM
McCall, James	Division 4, JM

McChesney, infant of J.R.	Division 4, IM (unmarked)
Meriwether, A.J. & Lorena	Division 22, AM
Meyer, Gus	Division 17, GM
Mitchell, Sallie & Thomas D., Sr.	Division 19, MI
Moffett, Ned & family	Division 18, MO
Morris, Ed family	Division 3, MO
Moss, Hubert & Annie	Division M, MO
Murrell, Gerry & Alex	Division V, MU
Murrell, Jesse & Ada	Division 4, MU
Nall, Sidney Robert	Division MA, SN
Nelson, James	Division 10, JN
Newton, Fred & Carmen	Division K, FN
Painter, D.L.	Division 19, DP
Parks, Bertie Lee	Division 21, BP
Parten, George Warren	Division S, GP
Patchell, Mary	Division 18A, SA
Peers, Val & Allie	Division 20, VP
Potter, Dixie & C.L.	Division 19, PO
Potter, Harold & family	Division 4, HP
Price, Jerry C.	Division 19, JP
Price, Margaret Mary	Division 19, JP
Price, Will	Division 8 (East of 7), WP
Pulliam, Richard	Division 11, RP (unmarked)
Ragsdale, G.H.	Division 1, GR
Ray, John	unknown grave location
Rigler, Lewis	Division 9, LR
Rose, Nora Hudson	Division 19, NR
Ross, Berlie Bolton & Ancil	Division 4, BR
Rumrill, Lady Edith	Division 3, LE
Rushing, Altie & Ida	Division 4, AR
Sanborn, Charles	Division 18A, SA
Schauseil, Theodore	Division 15, TS
Schiff, Henry	Division 24, HS
Schopmeyer, Henry	Division 21, HS
Scott, Bob & family	Division 18, SC
Scott, Rufus family	Division 2, SC
Simon, Elias	Division 4, ES
Simpson, George A., Sr.	Division 26, GS
Sims, David Lamont	Division J, DS

Sims, Russell W., Jr.	Division J, DS
Smith, Clyde	Division 11, CS
Smith, Morton & Mary Louise	Division O, MS
Steed, Jerry Lynn	Division 14, JS
Steverson, John	Division 23, JS
Stice, John	Division 18A, JS
Stokley, Edgar	Division 4, ST (unmarked)
Stone, J.B. family	Division 1, ST
Strong, Oregon & family	Division 18, ST
Stroube, Mary	Division 2, MS
Sugg, Eli Calvin & family	Division 19, SU
Sugg, J.D. "Ikard"	Division 19, SU
Sullivan, Edward	Division 11, ES
Sullivant, Carroll & Eloise	Division J, SU
Teague, Anna & Arthur, Sr.	Division V, AT
Thomason, Alice Culberson	Division XA, AT
Thomason, Belle Davis	Division 12, BT
Thurman, Lizzie	Division 21, LT
Timmis, Robert J., Sr. & family	Division 15, TI
Truitt, Mitchell	Division 7, MT
Turner, David	Division 14, TU
Turner, Ellie	Division 1, ET (unmarked)
Turner, Luther	Division 19, LT
Tuttle, W.H.M.	Division 17, WT
Tyler, F.A.	Division 21, TY
Vaeth, Maggie & Otto	Division 20, VA
Ware, H.P. "Pat"	Division 14, PW
Ware, Rad & Lula	Division 22, RW
Washington, James Russell, Jr.	Division V, JW
Washington, Josie & Jarrett	Division 4, JW
Wasson, Alonzo	Division 20, AW
Weaver, Agnes Darrah	Division 8 (East of 7), AW
Weaver, W.T.G. & Nancy	Division 4, WW
Whaley, J.O.A. family	Division 1, WH
Wheeler, John	Division 2, JW
Wilson, Nora	Division 14, NW (unmarked)
Woodruff, Dennis Hawkins	Division W, DW
Wright, Jake	Division 21, JW

Bibliography

Acheson, Sam Hanna. *Joe Bailey, the Last Democrat.* New York: Macmillan, 1932.

Allen, Tom. *Those Buried Texans: No Stone Unturned.* Dallas: Hendrick-Long, 1980.

Black History as Remembered by Black Gainesvilleites. Gainesville, TX: St. James CME Church, 1993.

Bush, A.E., and P.L. Dorman. *History of the Mosaic Templars of America: Its Founders and Officials.* Little Rock, AR: Central Printing, 1924.

California Medical Association. December 1950.

Cooke County (Texas) Clerk. *Records.*

Cooke County (Texas) District Court. *Records.*

Dallas Morning News.

Dyer, J.M. *History of Jefferson County, Oklahoma.* N.p.: 1957.

Gainesville Daily Register.

Gainesville Hesperian.

Gainesville Weekly Register.

Handbook of Texas Online.

Hunter, J. Marvin. *The Trail Drivers of Texas.* Nashville, TN: Cokesbury Press, 1925.

Jackson, Gwen. *Indians, Cowboys, and Homesteaders: From Pickens County to Grady County.* Privately published, 1998.

Larson, Leland A., and James R. Cook. *The Woodmen Story: "Our First 100 Years."* Omaha, NE: Woodmen of the World Life Insurance Society, 1991.

Leonard, Joe M., Jr. *Bah Bah Black Sheep.* Coral Springs, FL: Llumina Press, 2004.

Morris, John W. *Ghost Towns of Oklahoma.* Norman: University of Oklahoma, 1981.

Oklahoma Outlaws Lawmen History Association Online.

Powell, Shana. *Gainesville and Cooke County.* Chicago: Arcadia Publishing, 2000.

Powell, William F. *Cooke County History, Past and Present.* N.p.: Curtis Media Corporation, 1992.

Rigler, Lewis C., and Judyth Wagner Rigler. *In the Line of Duty: Reflections of a Texas Ranger Private.* Houston, TX: Larksdale, 1984.

Shirk, George H. *Oklahoma Place Names.* Norman: University of Oklahoma, 1974. 2nd ed.

Smith, A. Morton. *First 100 Years in Cooke County.* San Antonio, TX: Naylor Company, 1955; 2nd printing 1976.

Staniforth, Cora A. *A History of Cooke County, Texas in the World War.* Master's thesis, University of Texas, 1931.

Wood, Sue, and Ronnie Howser. *Fairview Cemetery: Gainesville, Cooke County, Texas.* Gainesville, TX: Cross Timbers Genealogical Society, 1985.

Works Progress Administration. *Oklahoma: A Guide to the Sooner State.* Norman: University of Oklahoma, 1941.

Index

D

U

V

W

X

About the Author

Ron Melugin has taught government and history at North Central Texas College in Gainesville for forty-five years. He has BA and MA degrees in history from Texas A&M–Commerce and has done graduate work at the University of North Texas. He is the historian for NCTC and is chair of the Cooke County Historical Commission, a local unit of the Texas Historical Commission. Melugin has done research for fourteen official Texas Historical Markers, six of which are in Fairview Cemetery in Gainesville. *Heroes, Scoundrels and Angels: Fairview Cemetery of Gainesville, Texas* is the culmination of approximately fifteen years of research. Melugin conducts historic tours of Fairview Cemetery regularly. This work allows the reader to conduct his own self-guided tour of this historic cemetery.